MANIC

Through Hell and Back

Terrelle T. Lewis

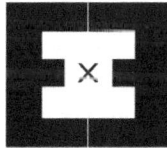

EXPECTED END

ENTERTAINMENT

Atlanta, GA

DEDICATION

I dedicate this book to every man, woman, and child who live with mental illness and the issues of life. I say to you all… go to God and He will show you who you are and what He wants you to do while you still have breath. Remember, *"Let everything that hath breath praise the Lord! Praise ye the Lord!"* Psalms 150:6

ACKNOWLEDGMENTS

I would like to acknowledge my mom, Ida Mae Brunson; my dad Gregory Allen Lewis; my brother Eric Lewis; my sisters Shannon Denise Rash/Lewis (my Partner in Christ) and LaNeeta Rochelle Berry/Lewis; my Brother Lorne Rash; all my nieces and nephews; Dave Smith; Stan Paul; my dear friends Larry Coleman, Reuben Coleman, Sara Coleman, Mrs. JoeNell Coleman, Mr. Larry Coleman, and Cindy Collins; Turtle Creek Valley Mental Health's Team: Dr. Uma, Donna, Debbie, Terra, Carol, and Dr. Jim Bieginni, Lou Anne; Klarque Garrison; and Chuck Brown. Special thanks to the love, motivation, and support of my wife Johnnette Young/Lewis who gave me the tools and push to complete the publishing of this book!

CONTENTS

INTRODUCTION

When I was a child, I was raised in a church where Hell was the most horrifying place of fire, terror, and torment. Unfortunately, I grew up fearing the devil and hell more than fearing God. It seemed that Hell was preached more than peace and prosperity. As I grew in age, so did my fear. Most churches always preached Hell's destination to those who live in sin. I grew up fearing life and making mistakes. I grew up being afraid of everything that could condemn me to Hell, so I developed emotional trauma and anxiety. I became depressed and frustrated with church, the devil, God, and everything that had to do with spirituality. Later in life, this frustration and depression turned into anger and aggression.

My thoughts were consistently preoccupied with fear and anxiety until I was put into different mental institutions over the years. I fought against my thoughts and sexual urges until one day I was diagnosed with manic depressant bipolar disorder. I loved being manic, but hated being depressed. My life became a constant rollercoaster of mental and physical mania. While family members and friends supported me, they could offer no true relief. I was hopelessly lost with no one to whom to turn until I finally submitted to the one being that I ran from for nearly two decades of my life. God gave me a revelation that changed my life from fear and torment into peace that surpassed my understanding.

I want everyone who reads this book to realize that God is real and He is only a prayer away from a life of peace and prosperity, a life of purpose and fulfillment. I sought out God through accepting the Holy Spirit of Jesus Christ and I have lived with greater understanding and peace of mind, more than I have ever lived. When you see the extreme happenings of my life and read the powerful change that God's love provided me, know that He can and will do the same for you.

"But seek ye first the Kingdom of God and His righteousness and all these things shall be added unto you!" Matt 6:33

HOW IT ALL STARTED

"For as a man thinks in his heart, so is he." I read those words in the Bible a long time ago and never quite grasped their true meaning. However, I believe that I experienced those words as a young adult and it might have been the most traumatic period of my life. I didn't know who I was nor did I have an identity. Some young men learn who they are by the example of their fathers. But for many, especially young African-American males, their fathers never show them this very crucial part of life because far too many are absent from the home. They're in jail, dead or have some other reason or excuse.

For me, I didn't want to be anything like my dad because he set an unacceptable example. The more I watched his lead the less I wanted to follow in his footsteps.

So I was forced to search out my own destiny by choosing the examples of friends and other men who I thought were prime examples of what a good man should be. And believe me, it wasn't easy.

I grew up in a household with two sisters and a brother. I was the second youngest. My mother and father never showed any signs of intimacy, at least none that I can remember. I was very close to my siblings when we were young but as we got older we seemed to grow apart. My parents separated when I was six, about the time I was baptized and accepted Christ into my life. My older brother followed, then my older sister. Like the rest of us, my younger sister was afraid to get baptized. I think she may have been confused by our parents' contradictory Christian lifestyle. We didn't see drug or alcohol abuse but we did see our father hit our mother from time to time.

Unfortunately, watching our parents' marriage come to an end caused us confusion about God and our search for Jesus Christ. By the time I turned 18, my brother had already graduated high school and my older sister studied the Koran. My younger sister got married a couple of years later and was raising a family of her own. I was the last to leave my dad's house. The day I decided to move in with my mother, a part of me stayed locked in my dad's house while the other part said, "Good riddance!"

My stay with my father was a great learning experience. My best friends, Luke and Ruach Median, meant the world to me. I had a crush on their older sister, Ester, who was and still is as beautiful as the morning sunrise. To me, their parents were the shining examples of God-fearing Christians. For a long time, I believed that no other family had a more intimate relationship with God. Mrs. Median took me under her wing and reintroduced me to Christ. Mr. Median was a man of few words and didn't speak to me much. But his actions were loud and clear. I grew so dependent on their love that other people seemed jealous of my relationship with them.

As time went on, so did my friends. Ruach graduated from Slippery Rock University, became a teacher and got married. Luke moved to Atlanta, Georgia, and is serving in the ministry as a deacon.

Before they moved, they saw a serious change in me. When I turned 21, I was high on life and had a lot of Bible knowledge. For years I had been faithfully studying at church and at Bible study with my friends but I never took it to heart. I believed in the idea of God without believing in God. My parents raised us in the church, but I could not fathom God's existence because I was preoccupied with my parents' depreciating relationship. God only aroused my intellect not my soul.

That was the main reason I developed anxieties and involuntary mental mania.

GOING MANIC

My most memorable and terrifying mental trauma was probably my first experience. One day during the early summer of 1992, I was going through the day with an unusually high amount of anxiety, stress, and fear. I left my mother's house fearing for my life and thinking that I was about to die and go to hell. In all the years learning about God, I was also studying the spiritual world and how the devil uses temptation to draw us away from God and uses the demons that he convinced to turn against the Most High. Consciously or unconsciously, I believed in the fear that consumed me more than the comforting Spirit of God and I couldn't find any relief from its relentless presence. Fear whispered to me that I would die if I did not receive the Holy Spirit that day.

Running aimlessly down the street to the bus stop, I headed for my church which was on the other side of town in the West End on Noblestown Road. As I waited downtown for the next bus, the people, the noise, and the traffic seemed nonexistent to me. I could only hear the voice in my head that kept saying, "Hurry up or you're dead!" I couldn't even find comfort in the words of the Bible that I clutched tightly as I rocked back and forth slipping farther and farther away from reality. I forgot about the other passengers on the bus and how I must have frightened them with my unusual behavior. Apparently, the bus driver was watching me, too, and had gotten annoyed. He warned me about my rocking back and forth and talking to myself, but I couldn't help it. The voice in my head was louder than my own and anyone else's. The bus driver was adamant about the passengers' safety and after two warnings he ordered me off the bus. I told him to keep driving. The last thing I heard the driver say was, "That's it! You're out of here!" He stopped the bus and grabbed my arm. "Nooooo!" I screamed jumping to my feet and running madly to the rear of the bus. I charged blindly and hit the rear wall and fell to the floor. With my eyes closed, I screamed for God's help because I felt no one else could. I heard the laughter and mockery of voices around me that forced my eyes open to see flaming red on everything. My eyes got wider as I looked through the windows and saw what looked like a modern day destruction of Sodom and Gomorrah. The trees and buildings were ablaze. Cars and telephone poles were consumed in fire. I quickly blinked several times and everything was back to normal. The sky was blue again and the people, the buildings, and everything else were as lovely as they should be. Yet when I blinked again, the flaming visions returned. A voice called out to me in a deep eerie tone and said, "Hey, it's okay. Stay calm." When I turned to look, I saw three red disfigured shapes coming towards me. "Come with us, please," the first figure said. I took them for demons and when he grabbed hold of my arm, it felt like my body was about to boil. "Get off me!" I screamed while pulling away. I fought hard for a moment, but was quickly overcome by forearms and nightsticks.

Bodies slammed down on top of me as I hit the floor. Hands grabbed at my neck and back, as my left foot bent backwards against my butt. They handcuffed my hands to my ankles. I struggled so hard that the cuffs tore into my flesh.

Suddenly, the figures hoisted me into the air, down the aisle, out through the doors, and into the heat of the afternoon sun. They threw me inside an empty metal vehicle face down and slammed the doors.

It was probably the scariest ride of my life. The bus had almost reached my church which sat atop Noblestown Road. So when the truck began its descent, I thought I was headed straight to hell. I bounced around inside that vehicle the entire ride. I could still hear the laughter and relentless mockery of voices. I could smell my blood that I sweated out like Christ in Gethsemane. My screams bounced off the walls inside the vehicle and back at me until it became intolerable.

Finally, the vehicle stopped and the doors flew open. I felt a blast of cool air hit my sweat-covered body while many hands secured me. I was slammed faced down onto a gurney and cuffed to its bars. My ankles were wrapped with bed sheets and tied to the bars as well.

The gurney smashed backwards through double doors and down the hallway. They yanked my pants down to my ankles and stuck a needle in my backside. As I struggled, I saw a pale shade of green upon everything. Suddenly, I yelled, "Shut up!" hoping to quiet the voices still mocking me. I was unable to stop the pain of the handcuffs on my bleeding wrists. I got lightheaded and exhausted, I assumed from the shot. I gave in to the soft gurney pad laying beneath me and laid my head on the pillow. The evil voices faded out and I could only hear the gentle, concerned voices of the doctors and nurses that surrounded me. I kept shutting my eyes and opening them expecting something else to happen.

WHERE AM I?

Am I in Hell?

Later, a tall African-American man with gray hair approached with a small white cup in his hand. He held it close to my lips. I sniffed the cup expecting to smell vinegar, but it was odorless. I figured an antagonist would offer someone in my state of mind vinegar like the Roman soldiers offered Jesus as he hanged on the cross. The man insisted I drink it, and since I didn't smell anything I sipped it until it was gone. It was water. He walked away and returned with more cool water. As I gulped down several cups, I felt a tight pinching on my shoulders and arms. Soon my entire body gave way to throbbing pains. As I lay my head back down on the pillow, I realized that I wasn't in hell but in a safe place with people not demons or creatures ready to torment me for all eternity.

My eyes got heavy but I glanced at my surroundings to see the color of the walls and the people. I breathed slowly and looked at the dried blood around my wrists. My eyes flooded with tears and I cried myself to sleep with one last thought... Forgive me, God, for not believing.

The next morning, I woke to the cries of my older brother. As I struggled to gain my balance, I felt like I had died and that God returned me to Earth because it wasn't my time. Unlike the day before, I felt an enormous amount of peace and a sudden sense of responsibility to my brother as he sat on the edge of the bed crying. He apologized for teasing and berating me in the past. I listened but I couldn't bear to hear him blame himself for what happened to me any longer.

"It's not your fault, Enoch. I'll be alright." I went back to sleep feeling sorrowful because I was unable to reassure my brother. The medicine that was injected into me the night before was still very potent. When I opened my eyes again, my brother was gone and the beautiful ray of sunlight that initially greeted me was too.

I opened the room door and wandered out into the strange facility. My body was heavy, but I felt safe. I saw people walking and talking to themselves while men and women in long white coats with clipboards and stethoscopes followed closely behind them. No one approached me as I took in my environment. I assumed the people dressed in street clothes were patients. The doctors that walked and talked to them were strange to me because they were in groups asking about the patient's feelings. Until that moment, I'd never seen doctors questioning patients as though they were clueless.

Meeting Victoria

I started thinking it must be some mental institution. Finally, a petite and quite attractive white woman approached me. Her hair came to the base of her neck. Her eyes were dark and beautiful. I studied the curve of her hips and backside.

She introduced herself as Victoria, a nurse, and I was a little shy when she looked at me. She took me to a small community room with other patients. I felt awkward standing there at six feet four inches with a puffy seven-inch afro while these peculiar people stared at me.

"Everyone, this is Terrelle," Victoria said. "He arrived last night and will be with us for a few days."

I gave a half grin and took a seat nearby. I didn't stare directly at anyone but as I scanned the room, I noticed the blank, sedative stares and the other patients' unusual demeanors. I could feel most of them trying not to notice me, but I must have been a giant to everyone and a little intimidating.

Victoria was about to start a group therapy session and asked if I wanted to join in. Although her beauty was inviting, I refused and returned to my room. I was looking for that peaceful awakening I had in my room when my brother was there earlier.

I stayed at this place for a week and endured many questions about drug abuse, my personal habits, emotional trauma, and other annoying questions. They offered medication, but I insisted that I didn't need any.

WHERE DO I GO FROM HERE?

Discharged: Going Home to the Same

When I was discharged, my best friend Luke was there to meet me. Although he was happy to see me, I couldn't look him in the eyes. I was embarrassed and ashamed. Even though Luke didn't show it, I knew he had a greater concern for me. He seemed more attentive to what I said and did. Feeling his eyes on me, even when I wasn't looking at him, made it worse.

After a few days, I began feeling scared and anxious. My mind raced and my heartbeat accelerated, including when I was trying to relax in the comfort of my bedroom. I wanted relief from these feelings but couldn't find an escape. My thoughts tormented me and I began hallucinating. A relapse seemed inevitable.

This experience was scarier than the first. Whispers tormented me all through the night. My head throbbed in agonizing pain. My brother was still asleep across the room. I didn't want to wake him so I quietly got up and went downstairs to the bathroom. I couldn't recognize my own reflection as I stared into the mirror. My eyes were dead and empty and my hair was matted and unkempt. I couldn't grasp reality's hand that seemed to dangle in front of me like a carrot leading a horse. I quickly filled with anxiety and rushed to the phone in my bedroom. My first thought was to call Pastor Levi, but he could no longer help me because he was in a backslidden state of mind. I called the next best person... his wife. The phone rang over and over again until finally someone picked up.

"Hello?" she said in her sweet voice.

"Mrs. Levi?" I cried as I begged for her response.

"Terrelle, are you ok?" she asked.

"Yeah. Mrs. Levi, could you give me a ride to church today?"

"Sure, I'll be there in about twenty minutes, ok?"

I didn't shower, brush my teeth, or comb my hair. I just threw on a decent pair of pants and a clean shirt. I couldn't wait for Mrs. Levi to pull up to my house and blow her horn. She and other members of her family were people that I could trust, but at that very moment, she was the only one I could trust.

My anxiety was so high that it tore through my soul like a lion. I felt the same way I did when I was on the bus and wanted to get to the church as soon as possible.

When she arrived, Mrs. Levi pushed open the passenger side door for me to get in. We didn't talk much. I knew she heard about my bus incident and knew something was wrong by the way I looked. I was mentally exhausted but I felt a little comfort from her presence.

Seeking the Holy Spirit's Help

When we arrived to the church, it looked like a different place. I looked at the walls and the stairway leading to the sanctuary. I gazed at the altar and the pulpit. Everything I looked at appeared larger and gloomier than I remembered and I felt oblivious to the few people that were there. I took a seat in the front pew and waited for the bishop to begin the sermon. I couldn't remember a single word of his sermon that day. All I wanted to hear was his prayer request at the end. I ran to the front seeking the Holy Spirit to fill me and for me to speak in tongues as evidence.

I closed my eyes trying to concentrate, but I was already

filled with doubt. Bishop Urnan placed his hand gently on my forehead and prayed. I prayed with him mumbling words of no meaning in the hope that the Holy Spirit would catch hold of my tongue, but the more I mumbled, the less I believed. My eyes remained closed and soon Bishop Urnan removed his hand and his voiced faded away from me.

After praying as hard and long as I could, I felt abandoned and dropped my head in despair. I kept my eyes closed but my soul kept longing for the Holy Spirit to fall upon me. I didn't know what to expect or how it would happen but I was sure it wasn't what was about to happen.

A voice returned before me and a hand returned to my forehead. But the voice came from higher than Bishop's voice. It was deeper and scarier, too. The voice terrorized me and I kept my eyes shut. It spoke with incredulous sarcasm as the words slid from his mouth like a forked tongue.

"Hallelujah, Hallelujah. Glory to God," he mocked.

I was scared. I began hearing more voices in the pews, despite the congregation being small and on this particular Sunday only about eight people were there. Those voices were loud and repulsive. I still hadn't opened my eyes but I continued to listen to what sounded like a crowd of obnoxious, ignorant drunkards. They sarcastically shouted the words to the song, "What a Mighty God We Serve". With my eyes still shut, I started seeing images of hell.

The floor fell away from me and the church walls turned to cave rocks with fire surrounding me. The voices singing became incoherent and turned to shouts of horror. At that point, I knew I was in hell with no chance at redemption. Everything around me was damnation and I felt a final farewell to my existence.

Moments later, the sounds subsided and I started feeling some peace. I reluctantly opened my eyes to an empty sanctuary and a vacant pulpit. I could see two figures standing in the rear doorway. As I stood there in fear, I looked but didn't recognize it was Mrs. Levi and Bishop Urnan. Their faces were distorted as were the surrounding structures. Everything looked strange and unfamiliar.

Where Do I Go From Here?

After several tries, Mrs. Levi and Bishop Urnan left the church, leaving me standing alone. I took a seat in the front pew, again waiting for a miracle or some type of sign from God. But nothing happened. I grew tired of the silence so I decided to leave the safety of the sanctuary and walk down the stairs to the outside doors. I pushed them open and peeked outside. The street was quiet and empty. I was the last to leave and as I walked down the street, every building, tree, and rock looked fake to me. I felt like I was in the Land of Oz except there were no beautiful colors or yellow brick road to follow. I wondered if I slipped into eternity where there was no time, no beginning, or end. My thoughts were so entangled that I couldn't tell what time of day it was or which direction to take.

I embarked on a long journey home because I had no trust in anyone I saw. Bishop's car drove past me toward the church. I walked back towards the church, but I was too far to stop him from locking the doors. He didn't say anything to me. He walked to the church doors, locked them, returned to his car, and left.

I stood there as he drove by me and down the street. I felt abandoned and isolated. I continued back down the street, cautiously observing everything. I watched as a black and white couple trudged by me in the opposite direction. They hesitantly looked at me and moved on. A few minutes later, I saw what appeared to be the same couple walking again in the opposite direction. I slowed my pace and stared at them as they approached. They walked towards me with caution then passed by. I concluded that they were ghosts and that I was either one as well or that my mind had developed the ability to see them.

I came to the parkway exit of the West End Bridge. I walked to the side and down the ramp onto the Parkway East. Suddenly, I found myself surrounded by speeding traffic honking and swerving past me. I had really thought I was a ghost but at that moment I realized my time had not quite come yet. As cars got closer and horns got louder, I got scared. I could feel the breeze as cars raced past me and slammed on breaks to avoid me. I extended my arms in a sign of submission to my demise, thinking that I was about to be smashed from behind by one of these metal monsters. The traffic was loud and frightening but the voice I heard was even worse.

"Hey you! Get over here! What the hell's the matter with you?!"

I looked over to my left and saw an older African-America police officer and a police car. I felt a sense of relief because he could see and hear me. I walked over to him knowing that he had just saved my life. He cuffed my already scared wrists and shoved me in the back of his patrol car. The pain from the handcuffs shot through me like an arrow and the heat from the afternoon sun made me feel like a prisoner of war.

"What's your name?" the officer said. "What's your name!?!"

"Terrelle, Terrelle Lewis."

"What's wrong with you, boy?" he asked in an angry tone.

"I don't know," I said while he connected my handcuffs to a restraining bar in the center of the back seat.

When the officer had me locked in, he radioed in my arrest. I felt like I was dreaming. Everything was pale and dull. Nothing around me looked real.

HEADED BACK TO HELL

Headed Back to Hell

As he pulled off, I didn't care where he was taking me. I assumed he was taking me to the police station so I just sat back and enjoyed the ride. I looked out the window at the ambient scenery. I felt like I was in hell again.

Later, we arrived at the police station where he unlocked the cuffs briefly and led me to a holding room. There were about four or five other officers there that made me feel a little uncomfortable. The officer cuffed me to a restraining bar in the floor and sat me in a chair while he walked behind a desk and filled out papers. I sat there and tugged gently at my restraints.

My anxiety returned as I overheard the officers talking about me. The one officer came over, unlocked my cuffs and led me to a phone that was off the hook. I picked it and spoke quietly, "Hello?"

"Terrelle, what's wrong?"

It was my mother. She spoke in a very soft but concerned voice.

I knew it couldn't be her because we were in hell.

"Mom...where are you?"

"I'm at home, baby. What's wrong?"

I couldn't speak any further. I didn't want them to bring her down here with me. I concluded that I was trapped in hell and that the officers were demons in human form waiting to catch my family and friends and trap them down here with me. I blamed myself for everything that was happening. I believed that I had to protect everyone I knew from being deceived by sin but I had no idea how to accomplish this great and terrible burden.

Time seemed to speed by when I was being taken back to the psychiatric institution. It was dusk before I knew it and when I reached the floor of the psych ward, my surroundings were a lot more eerie than the first time I was there. Two large men escorted me to a different room. I felt so lost, so afraid.

As I passed some of the patients, one of them mocked me saying, "Welcome back, Terrelle! Ha Ha Ha."

They took me to a dark room with no lights. A small, scary looking man sat on the bed. He had a low and deceptive voice. He talked with his fingers outstretched at me. His words slid off his tongue like a snake. As I stared at him, his eyes seemed to glow red and his face kept changing shapes. I disliked him immediately and took him for the spirit of fear. I was afraid when I looked at him but tried not to show it. The doctors called him out the room but before he left I grabbed his arm and through gritted teeth said, "Stay away from me!" He stared into my eyes and gave an evil smirk, giggled, yanked his arm from me, and walked out. I was furious that my giant stature didn't scare him and I realized that I was on foreign grounds.

I followed after him with the intent of punching him in the back of his head but security guards stopped me.

Most of the patients on this floor were too afraid of their own thoughts to be afraid of me. I felt completely vulnerable on this floor and became claustrophobic. I asked the nearest person who looked like an employee if I could stay in the room I was in during my first visit to this hospital. I was told it was already occupied.

My thoughts raced. I almost had another anxiety attack until I spotted Victoria, the nurse from my first stay there. I instinctively gave her a gentle hug and felt safe. Not feeling that way with anyone else, I tried to remain by her side as often as I could and she attended to me a lot.

The next morning my brother and younger sister came through the visitor's entrance and raced towards me. I tightly held both of them as tears streamed down my face. It was hard to keep a thought in my head while they were there. There was no hiding who I was and who I was becoming. Unfortunately, nobody knew what was wrong with me, not even the doctors or nurses. My brother and sister repeatedly said, "You'll be all right." Although they meant well, their words gave me no comfort. I was experiencing something I had never felt before and I wanted immediate healing.

Diagnosed Bi-Polar

The doctors labeled me bipolar. The pain of not knowing what is was overtook me and I didn't want my family seeing me this way. I stood tall and told them to go home. My brother, of course, refused. He was always the one with strong affirmation.

"Get out!" I yelled while walking to my room.

I really didn't want them to leave but I didn't want them in my presence either. I walked into my room, pushed the door shut, and dropped to my bed as a man condemned. Minutes later, my brother slowly pushed the door open and called to me.

"Rell, you ok?"

"Yeah." I grumbled.

I knew that things would never be the same between my family and me. My issues had finally surfaced and the emotional impact was going to affect us all. My brother gently put his hand on my shoulder and slowly embraced me. I didn't hug him back. He said in a low, concerned voice, "We'll come back tomorrow, ok?"

"Yeah, ok."

I couldn't look at him anymore. He stood briefly over me and said, "See ya." As he left the room and closed the door behind him, I sat on the edge of my bed crying as the pale moonlight shined into the room. The idea of my condition weighed on me and I felt my life taking a dramatic detour from those I love dearly. Part of me wanted to run after my brother and stop him from leaving, but I didn't.

I sat in my room expecting to hear the voices again or the sound of mocking laughter that tormented me before. There was nothing. I could barely hear the voices of the many nurses and patients that were still on the floor. I didn't realize how tired I was. After all, I did spend most of the afternoon walking from the West End to the Parkway East. I lay my head down on the pillow and relaxed.

THE LARGE PINK PILL

The Large Pink Pill

I thought that the staff had forgotten about me until I heard a quiet knock on my room door. I was hoping it was my brother returning to comfort me but I was wrong.

"Terrelle, are you all right?"

"No!" I said to the unfamiliar voice.

"Will you do me a favor and swallow this pill?"

"What's it for?" I asked with resistance.

"It's just a sedative to calm you down."

"I'm already calm!" I said with anger.

"Are you sure? Because I could get someone to help you take it," she responded.

After a few seconds I realized that she just threatened me. "Is that bitch trying to scare me or something?" I thought.

I shouted back at her: "I don't care!"

"Ok!" she said.

Moments later, the bedroom light came on and I rolled over to behold a scraggly, gray-haired, heavyset woman who looked like a witch. Three large men the size of professional wrestlers accompanied her. She flashed an arrogant grin and said, "You want to take this pill now, Terrelle?"

I looked at them briefly then turned my back to them. Suddenly, a large hand gripped the back of my neck, pulled me up and turned me around. The other two guards sat on either side of me with latex gloves on and held my arms down to my sides. They didn't say a word but my struggling made their heavy breathing sound like a pack of wild dogs fighting over a piece of meat. The nurse walked toward me with an evil grin and held a small Dixie cup in one hand and a clear plastic cup with a large pink pill in the other. I was enraged by their use of excessive force and I wrestled with them, realizing they were about to force feed me this pill.

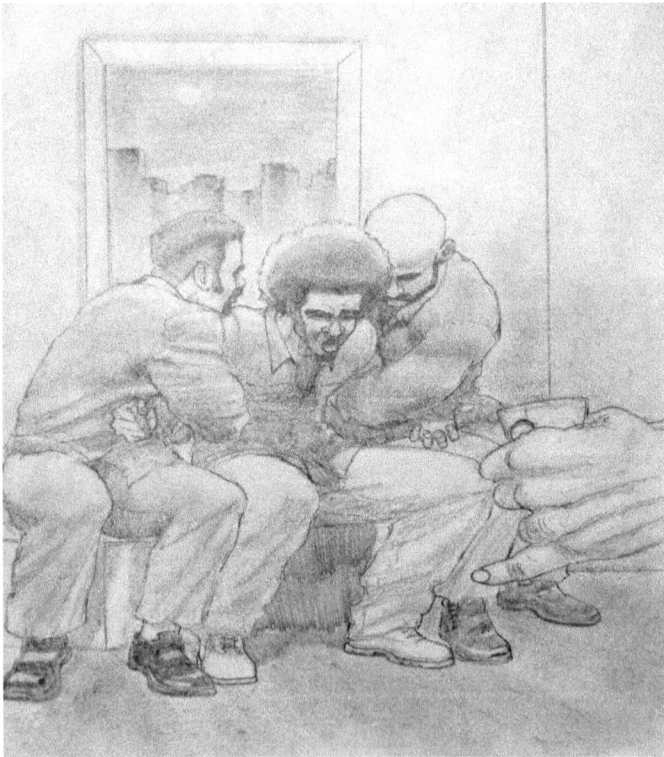

"Get off me!" I yelled.

"Terrelle, you have to calm down. This isn't going to hurt you. We just want you to relax and get some sleep," the nurse said.

"I don't need your stupid pill to fall asleep!"

I don't know where I found the strength, but I stood up, lifting the guards with me to their surprise. As they tried to restrain me, my anger was kindled. Everything turned pale green and I returned to the overwhelming thoughts of survival. I fought like I was being attacked by monsters from a nightmare. I hadn't realized that I had overcome one security guard while fighting off another. The nurse screamed and ran out the room. I saw her as my enemy and took off after her. One of the guards blocked my path but I was too angry to allow anyone to deter my actions. I rammed headfirst into the guard's chest and lifted him through the doorway.

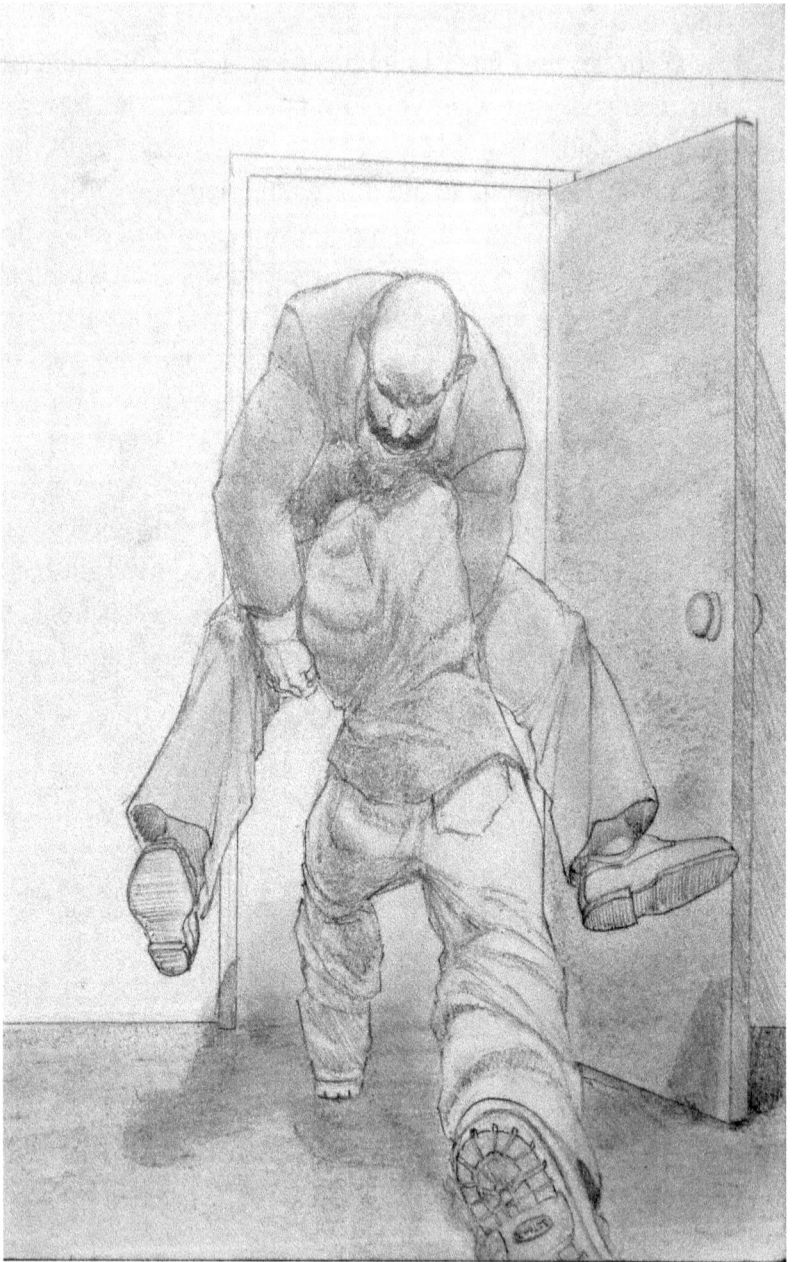

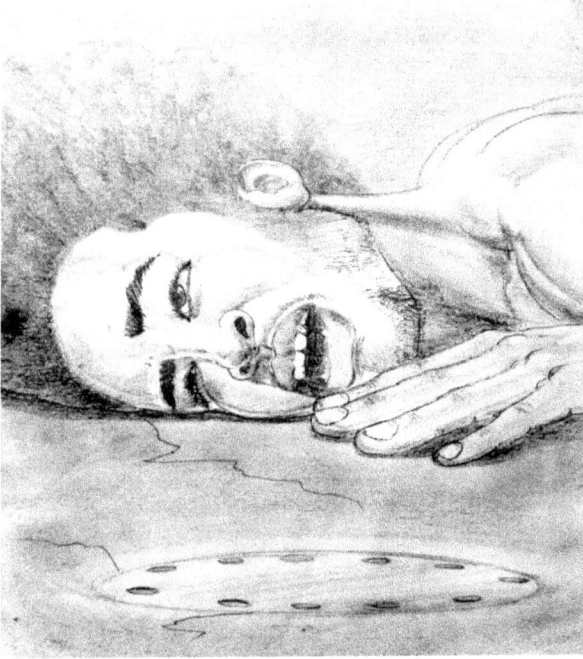

My next memory was my hands around the guard's neck and then a sudden blow to the back of my head. I was overcome by extreme vertigo and fell to the floor.

I woke up in a small room with a twin-sized green mattress on the floor next to me and a drain hole in the middle of the floor. A small, square-shaped light in the ceiling repeatedly got brighter and dimmed. I was naked. There was a large pair of pajama bottoms lying on the floor so I put them on. The room was so hot that I could barely stand and the flickering lights didn't help.

I lost consciousness again and woke up the next day still in that room. I walked over to the door and looked out a small square window.

There was a nurse and doctor on the other side. I knocked on the window to gain their attention. They looked briefly then continued talking to each other. I could hear them faintly but couldn't understand a word they were saying. They were both writing on small notepads and gesturing towards the window at me. I tried reading their lips but I had a terrible headache from the blow I received from the guard a few days earlier. I couldn't take my attention off them because they appeared concerned.

Another door behind them slowly opened and four large security guards lumbered in with gray pants and blue blazers. I got concerned as they approached my door. I backed away to the rear wall of the room as the guards walked towards me with the nurse and doctor following. I looked between the guards at the doctor and nurse. It was the same guards. I remembered their faces after a while. I was getting sick of them. They cornered me as I stood with my back against the wall. I gave them my one and only warning to stay away from me but they continued to approach. I stood there half-naked remembering the fear of going to hell. I suddenly had a will to survive.

When the closest guard reached for my arm, I maneuvered out of his grip. He didn't take my denial with grace. He grabbed at my arm again like a father takes hold of a disobedient child but I used his back as a battering ram as I charged forward slamming him, the nurse, and the doctor against the other wall.

The other security guards rushed in and took me down, holding my arms in a full nelson. They held my legs while the nurse slowly approached with a large pink pill. As the pill cup approached my lips, I jerked back hitting the guard in the face with the back of my head. I felt something warm on my neck and realized that I must have busted his mouth or nose. It was my final act of desperation before the guards had enough of my outbursts. They threw me to the ground and hit me in the head and shoulders knocking the wind out of me. I screamed as the nurse took the opportunity to drop the pill into my mouth. The guards set me up and held my nose forcing me to swallow.

I hacked and coughed until the nurse gave me water. The injured guard stood up then shoved the side of my head and I fell back to the floor. He was the last person I saw before I closed my eyes.

I don't know if it was the pill or the punches that caused me to pass out but I was left with a nasty taste in my mouth for the next few hours. I kept trying not to fall asleep as my cheek and chest lay on the cold floor. I kept my eyes open long enough to see feet leaving the room. I noticed that the last guard left the seclusion door open. The light dimmed to the awful color of the room and I could no longer bear its appearance so I closed my eyes for a while.

Almost Free?

"Terrelle!" a voice whispered.

"Huh?" I said as I opened my eyes. "Who's that?"

"The door's open!" the voice said. "Go!"

I slowly stumbled to my feet and pushed at the door. It didn't open. I threw a stiff shoulder into it and jolted it open then caught the door before it hit the wall. I crept out of my personal prison to the main door of the seclusion rooms.

This was my way to freedom but the doorknob wouldn't budge. I was frustrated. I stepped across the floor with mouse-like quietness looking for something to pick the lock. There, way in the corner, a shiny piece of metal. I wondered if it was a key. But it was a piece of metal from the doctor's stethoscope. It must have broken off when I fought with the guards. I picked it up and examined it. It was smooth on one side and rough on the other. I tried to shape a key-like figurine to pick at the lock. I jiggled it around inside the key hole and tried turning the knob relentlessly. Sweat poured down my face and into my eyes, but I never blinked. I continued prying at the doorknob for about 20 minutes until, finally, I heard a click and the doorknob turned. I opened the door slowly and peeked out into the hallway. It was the middle of the night and everyone was in their rooms. There were no doctors or nurses, just a dark hallway with dimly lit ceiling lights in both directions. I saw a brighter light glowing from down the hall.

I tip-toed towards the light and found that it was from the elevator. It had been propped open with an ink pen shoved into the rubber seems of the doors. I entered the elevator, removed the pen and pushed the basement floor button. With the slow descent, my head pounded and I began to feel a swirl of vertigo and nearly passed out.

When the doors opened, I looked into a dark room filled with dirty linen, slippers and scrubs. I searched for a set of scrubs that I could fit and some slippers. While I was squirming into a scrub shirt, an alarm sounded that nearly stopped my heart. The elevator ascended to the upper floors and I quickly threw on the scrub bottoms.

I saw a door in the rear of the room that had a traffic cone and caution tape in front of it. I kicked the cone aside and ran through the caution tape, kicking the doors open. I entered another room with caution tape stretched everywhere. Without hesitation, I charged through the tape and rammed through the doors. The early morning air hit me like a Mack truck but the parking lot was a quick fifty-yard dash before I entered the woods. Ducking and dodging branches and leaping over tree roots, I raced through the woods, instinctively making a path to an unknown destination. I felt like a runaway slave and was expecting to hear the sounds of blood hounds chasing me.

"Terrelle!" a voice cried out. "This way!"

I looked around but didn't see anyone.

"This way!" the voice repeated.

I followed the voice as it led me out of the woods onto a narrow road and into an abandoned building.

"Stay here!" the voice said in a concerned tone.

"Where are you?" I asked as I stared into the black empty room.

"I'm here," it said.

"Where?"

"Just be quiet and listen!"

I waited for more direction from the voice. Instead, I heard faint sounds of sirens and police bands. Soon the sounds of authority faded until there was nothing more than the defining sound of absolute silence.

"You're ok, just stay calm. Are you hungry?"

"Why?" I asked.

"I'll get you something to eat."

I didn't expect anything from the voice even though it sounded familiar. I felt like I had to continue acknowledging it. I tried repeatedly to put a face to the voice but could find no referrals. Finally I became apprehensive and I shouted, "Shut up! You can't get me nothin'!"

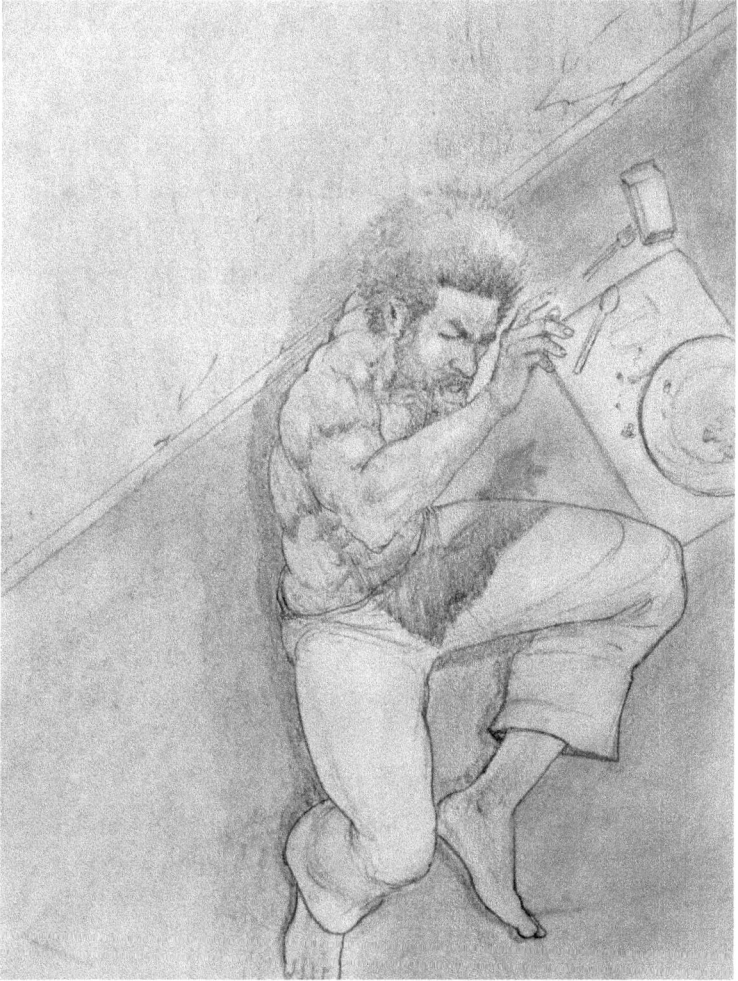

As soon as I rejected the voice, I smelled the pleasant aroma of pancakes and syrup with scrambled eggs and cinnamon. My curiosity brought me to my feet in the pitch black room. I took a step forward and followed the smell but my first step met a mushy soft surface and I realized that I had stepped on my meal. I stepped back, sat down and removed my food-covered slipper. I reached in front of me and felt around until I found a tray full of pancakes, sausages, eggs and toast. I shoved the food into my mouth with no regard for utensils until it was all gone. I needed something to wash down the food so I stretched out my arm over the tray and knocked over a cold carton of what I assumed was milk. I was so thirsty that I ripped it open with my teeth and poured the milk into my mouth. I pawed the tray to see if I missed anything then leaned back against the wall and sat briefly with content.

After a few minutes, I sat up and realized that I had to find my way home.

"Hey, hey you...where you at?" I said.

"I'm here," the voice replied.

"What's next?"

"Well, you can get a shower and comb your hair."

"What!?!"

"...And after you take your medication, you can watch television, ok?"

"Wait a minute, who are you?"

As I lifted my head, I saw a blinding light and heard voices surrounding me. My face was covered with eggs, syrup and drool. As I pushed myself off the floor, I felt aches and pains on my chest and knees. The "nurse witch" was standing over me with four large men in dark blue blazers. They had on latex gloves and the nurse carried a clear cup with a large pink pill in one hand and a cup of water in the other. I slowly stood and took in my surroundings. I was standing in the isolation room where they had put me days earlier. When I realized that I must have been dreaming, I got very angry.

I couldn't have dreamt it, I thought. It seemed so real. I

had a migraine and I was weak, still feeling like I was hit by a truck.

"Where am I?" I asked again.

"You're in the seclusion room at the hospital, Terrelle," the nurse said.

"What? Nah, man I thought I was... outside... or... something. No I was... I was..."

The nurse walked towards me cautiously and spoke in a soft, caring tone. She seemed more frightened of me this time but she continued closer. The guards surrounded us while cracking their knuckles and fingers and loosening their neck muscles to intimidate me.

"Terrelle, do you remember me? I'm Ms. Francine," the nurse said.

I didn't say a word. I was angry that I was still in isolation when I just knew that I was almost free.

"Do you know where you are?" she said. "You're in the seclusion room at Western Psychiatric Hospital. You were nonresponsive after we administered an advanced level of medication. Apparently you remained in a catatonic state for three days until the medication finally wore off. The headaches and confusion are side effects. They will pass in time, but you must continue taking the medication in order for you to get better."

"Medication," I said in a low deep voice. "I didn't take any medication except for when you forced it down my throat."

"I know and I'm sorry, Terrelle. But you were a bit out of control," she said taking a step back.

I wiped the eggs and drool from my face and tried to maintain a defensive posture while she kept trying to keep me calm.

"We're gonna give you a smaller dosage so you can get cleaned up, ok?" she said.

I stood there with my head down and my peripherals on the guards who continued closer to me. I didn't respond to the nurse and for a moment we all stood there in silence.

"Will you take the pill for me, please?" she asked.

I didn't respond. I stood there thinking about the last fight I had with the guards and I was anticipating another one. But I was too weak and in too much pain.

"Come on, Terrelle!" the closest guard said as he grabbed my left arm. His grip was strong and hard on the bruises I had from fighting them earlier. I was about to take a swing with my right arm but the pain was overbearing. He gripped even harder when I refused to comply.

"Ahh shit!" I grumbled.

"Come on, son!" the guard repeated.

Another guard took hold of my other arm causing more pain to shoot through my body. I was so angry that I didn't have enough strength to fight them. I just dropped to the floor as my last desperate attempt to deny the large pink pill. The nurse saw her opportunity and kneeled down with the pill while the guards crouched down on either side of me restraining my arms. She pushed the cup to my lips but I folded them in and turned away.

One of the guards gripped the back of my head and straightened it to her. She grabbed my cheeks and squeezed saying, "Open up! Open up!" I opened my mouth and sank my teeth into her index finger. She screamed, dropping the pill in my lap and fell backwards to the floor and cried. I didn't have a chance to be remorseful. The guard to my right grabbed my face and slammed my head back against the wall.

"That's enough outta you boy!" he said.

They turned me face down on the floor and punched me in the head and shoulders knocking the wind out of me. They tore off my soiled pajamas and left me naked on the floor. I lay there moaning in pain wondering how I was caught. I was sure I had escaped from that God-forsaken madhouse.

LEARNING ALONG THE WAY

Finding Hope

After the sound of the seclusion door opening woke me, I felt a cool breeze sweep over my aching body. I heard a voice and saw a familiar face; it was Victoria. She stood over me brushing her hand gently across my forehead. Her eyes gave a concerned, yet inviting stare. The four guards stood around her and close enough to me to make sure I was no threat. She was the only one that I complied with and the only one that I was glad to see.

"Terrelle," she said." Do you remember me?"

I lay there groaning but I was so pleased to see her. Her beautiful brown eyes and shiny red lipstick along with her soft glowing skin were like being awakened by an angel.

"Can you get up? I have some clean pajamas for you. I want you to come with me and get showered, ok?" she said.

I let out a loud groan and said, "Yeah!" The guards lifted me off the floor. The guard that slammed my head against the wall smirked and said, "Sorry about your head." I'll never forgot that pretentious smirk. The nurse guided my legs into the pajamas and fastened them for me. The guards relaxed their grip and allowed me to stand on my own, but my legs were too weak and they caught me before I fell. My head was spinning and the lights hurt my eyes. I got nauseous and irritable.

"Why am I so tired?" I asked.

"When you were catatonic the doctors continued your medication, but they were unable to administer the correct dosage for a man of your size," she said. "You may still be experiencing auditory and visual hallucinations and delusions, but they will pass in time."

"So what's gonna happen? Am I gonna get better?"

"You'll be fine. You just have to take the medication so you can get better."

"What's wrong with me?"

"You've been diagnosed with manic depression bipolar disorder."

"Bipolar? What the hell is bipolar?"

"It's a condition in the brain that generally affects the mood. You're lacking certain chemicals in your brain and the medication will help regain the proper balance."

"I don't need your drugs! I never used drugs in all my life. I hate swallowin' pills and shit!"

"Terrelle, listen, you're in a very confused state of mind and the medication will help you with that, ok? Now come on, trust me!"

I was mesmerized by her beautiful face, framed by her short black hair. Her angelic eyes cast shiny sparkles of bluish green. Her voice was like a concerned mother or wife so I agreed. The guards kept me lightly retrained even though I was in no condition to struggle anyway. They led me out the seclusion room and onto the patient floor.

The bright morning sun shined through the windows of the open bedroom doors and onto the hallway carpet. Patients slowly crawled out their beds and many of them froze in their doorways when they saw me being escorted down the hall with the guards following closely.

I was glad to be out of seclusion and feeling the soft warm carpet below my feet. The smell of food still lingered in the air and the company of people around me gave me a submissive attitude. I didn't want to go back to isolation so I didn't give them any reason to put me back there.

In the three days I had been in isolation, there were some new faces among the patients. Although they stared as if I had a third eye on my forehead, I didn't care. I didn't try to frighten them either. I just wanted to blend in and enjoy the environment of social order on the patient floor. At that point, only two things gave me comfort – the smell of breakfast and the pretty nurse.

As we walked down the hall, I glanced at her curvy hips and butt and suddenly realized that I hadn't had a sexual thought in a long time.

"What's your name?" I asked.

"My name is Victoria. Don't you remember me from the first time?"

"Victoria, nice to meet you."

I extended my hand but the guards warned her of my potential danger.

"It's all right," she said. She took my hand. "It's nice to meet you again."

With a smile she said, "Come on honey, let's get you cleaned up!"

She stood in the bathroom doorway while the guards watched closely outside. I turned my back to her as I got undressed, feeling insecure. Before I was committed, I worked out five days a week. Unfortunately, the doctors would not allow me to leave the floor for any reason other than diagnoses and mental tests or analyses. My physical appearance was, for me, unacceptable so I politely asked her not to look at me. She turned away and extended her arms to give me soap, shampoo, and a clean set of pajamas. My movements were slow and mechanical. I felt like a newborn calf struggling to his feet while learning how to walk. The more I wobbled about for strength and coordination, the more frustrated I became.

Finally, I turned the shower on and put my hand under the faucet waiting for the warmth to hit my hand. It seemed like it took about 10 minutes to get to a comfortable temperature and another 20 minutes to stand in the shower's orgasmic warm wet spray.

"Are you ok, Terrelle?" Victoria asked.

"Yeah!" I said in a moan of pleasure.

"Let's get you dried off soon."

I acted as though I didn't hear her but I began to squeeze the shampoo on top of my head and scratch its moisture through my coarse nappy hair. I never felt so much delight when washing my hair before. Victoria called to me again and I returned a gentle, "Ok... Ok... I'm coming." I stood in the shower a while longer. I had an extremely hard erection. I hadn't had a single hedonistic thought for weeks so I fantasized about Victoria and masturbated. I saw her in extreme amatory positions and imagined her climaxing with me. I almost forgot how good that felt. I felt like a new man for a moment. After I ejaculated and cleaned off, I felt the sting of guilt and embarrassment.

I slowly dressed and emerged from the bathroom. I couldn't look Victoria in the eyes. If black people could blush, I would've given myself away. I held my soiled pajamas against my crotch and walked down the hallway behind Victoria as the guards walked closely behind me. The other doctors and patients gawked as if I were a criminal on death row. Finally, Victoria led me to the room that I was in on my first visit. I probably would've been content but there was a small problem. The creepy man I pegged for a spirit of fear was my roommate. He sat on the bed I used during my first stay. My countenance fell as I slowly walked in.

"This is Richard, Terrelle. He's going to be your roommate for a while," Victoria said.

"A while?" I said. "How long am I gonna be here?"

"Well, you're going to be here until you get better."

I couldn't take my eyes off Richard. He never took his off me either and that bothered me. He showed no fear of me. Quite truthfully, he frightened me.

"Man, why he gotta be in here? I want my own room!" I said.

"I know but we're short of space," Victoria said.

With his beady red eyes and a smirk on his face, Richard stared at me. I searched for an emotion that would comfort me, but my thoughts were everywhere and my head still ached.

Suddenly, my mind found an indignant memory that gave me strength and I kept this thought in my head every time fear came upon me.

"Hiya Terrelle," Richard said in a deep voice.

I angrily responded, "Man, don't say nothin' to me! Dog, I ain't playin'!"

Victoria tried to jump in to diffuse the situation. "What's wrong, Terrelle?"

"Nah, man, I don't like that muthafucka!" I said.

"What's your problem?" Richard asked.

"A yo, shut up!" I said.

"Ok, ok, Terrelle, calm down," Victoria said. "We'll find you another room."

"Nah, make *him* leave!" I said.

After I raised my voice, Victoria quickly moved past me and out the bedroom door. Within seconds, the guards entered. "What's the problem, Terrelle?" one of the guards said.

I got the feeling that these same four guards were getting tired of dealing with me.

"Yeah, man, get his punk ass outta here... That's the problem!" I said.

"Well, we can't do that right now. But I'll tell you what. Why don't we put you back into the seclusion room? Would you like that?" the guard said.

I turned toward the guard and saw the evil grimace upon his face. He moved toward me as if he had the intentions of beating me to a pulp. At first, I was nervous but then I remembered the thought that gave me strength in times of fear. I thought about the "witch nurse" trying to force me to take that medication. I remembered how angry I got and how I rammed one of the guards through the doorway. I forgot what I was capable of when I'm consumed with anger.

I wasn't that angry at the guards. I was very tired and simply wanted to relax outside of the seclusion room.

"Come on, good buddy! Let's get you back to the seclusion room," the guard said.

He extended his arm and snapped his fingers, motioning for me to come with him. That was an insult to me so I refused.

"What's that son?" he said. "I didn't hear you?"

"Yes you did!" I fired back.

I took a defensive posture and tightened my fists. I knew I couldn't win, but Richard was still sitting on the edge of the bed staring excitedly as if he were watching a title bout. If anything were to happen, I couldn't show any fear. Maybe then Richard would fear me, I hoped.

"Well now, Terrelle, looks to me like we have a failure to communicate," the guard said. "Let's talk about it on the way to the seclusion room."

Suddenly, the damp smell of that seclusion room hit me like a ton of bricks. As the guard reached for my arm, I smacked it away.

"Now you listen to me, boy!" the guard said.

Again, Victoria tried to jump in and diffuse the situation.

"Stop!" she yelled. "I'll handle this gentlemen."

With a concerned look on her face, she walked towards me, took me by the hand and bid me to sit on the bed with her. I squeezed her hand as I walked with her, still keeping my eyes on Richard who sat on the other bed with that stupid grin on his face.

"Whatchu lookin' at, punk?" I said.

"Terrelle! Take it easy, honey! Why are you so angry with Richard?" Victoria said.

"Cause he keep starin' at me like some faggot or somethin'!" I said.

"Terrelle, that's not nice. Richard is here for the same reason as you," she said.

"Yeah, whatever. If he keep lookin' at me like that I'm goin' beat his ass! That's all I'm sayin!"

Turning to the guards, Victoria said, "Guards, will you take Richard outside for a second, please?"

"Yes ma'am," they replied.

My eyes didn't leave Richard until the door closed behind them.

As Victoria and I sat in the empty room, I had a sense of peace, the same peace I felt when my brother was there. Victoria talked to me without fear or hostility. It was as if she had known me for a long time. She was always attentive and accommodating and that's why I trusted her. She gently held my hand and said, "I want you to know that you're in a safe place and no one is going to hurt you."

"Yeah," I said in a low voice. I looked at the bruises on my arms and rubbed the scars on my wrists from the handcuffs. She followed my eyes to my scars and whispered, "What happened?"

"The guards beat me up."

"Why? What happened?"

"I can't remember. I think it was because I didn't want to take their medication. They tried to force me to take it and whooped my ass in the process."

"Oh dear! Are you ok?"

"Yeah, I'm cool. Wait 'til I tell my mom!"

"Has she come to visit you yet?"

"No. I really don't want her to come."

"Why not?"

"I don't want her to see me like this."

"Well I'm sure she wants to see you. Maybe when she comes to visit, you can talk to her about... well... I don't know... whatever."

"Yeah... whatever!"

She brushed the side of my face with her hand and stared at me for a moment. I slowly turned to her and when my eyes met hers, I was terrified. I knew my thoughts were impure but all I could do was turn away.

"Terrelle, listen! I'm here until 2:30 so until that time if you need anything, ask for me and I'll see if I can accommodate you. Ok?"

"Ok. Thanks, Ms. Victoria."

"You're welcome!"

As she stood to leave, I took her into my arms and gently embraced her. I was a little worried that she might have gotten afraid and pushed me away. But I felt her arms gently squeeze my waist. I let her go, opened the door and followed her out. The guards were still standing outside the door, each with a different expression on his face. As they looked at me, my smile must have made them uneasy. Victoria walked through them expressionless.

"Is everything all right, ma'am?" one of the guards said.

"Everything's fine," she said. "Can I see you guys in the office, please?"

They adjusted their ties and blazers and followed her.

I suddenly remembered Richard but when I turned to confront him, he was already gone.

Adjusting to the Surroundings

The days there were long and terribly boring. I only knew the time of the day by the meal schedule. As the seasons changed, I grew more depressed. I was isolated from my family and just wanted to get out of that place. But with each passing day, it seemed like that would never happen.

Sometimes I found myself scared and anxious, but when I saw other patients, their behavior and appearances, I laughed and felt like my old self again. I was convinced that there was nothing wrong with me but the doctors and nurses reiterated my confused state, especially with the large pink pill.

I got restless, especially after dinner. I missed my family, especially my brother. That was usually the time I congregated with other patients instead of isolating myself. Three months went by and I had gained about 20 pounds from lack of exercise and motivation. Every time I looked into the mirror, I was disgusted. My hair was matted and nappy and my beard was wild and thick like a squalid bush.

I walked up and down the hallway just to deal with the sorrow. Even though I didn't speak to anyone, I was entertained by the other patients.

My mom and dad visited me about five or six times within those three months but I never mentioned my fighting with the guards to either of them. Even though I wanted to tell them, I felt that holding back that information gave me a small sense of courage and inner strength.

Making a Friend

After I was discharged, I kept running into former patients. They were easy to recognize in the hospital but in public some of them blended in well. Others stood out like a sore thumb. Take Maurice, for example, a 6'6" 295-pound black man from the Hill District. He had a heavy, but solid stature with unkempt hair. When I first met him, I was about to be discharged from my first visit. He looked at me and was convinced that I could read his mind. He often asked me how I knew what he was thinking. He referenced the Bible a lot and since I knew many of the verses, he thought I was reading his mind. I told him that nobody but God had that ability.

When I returned to the psyche institute the second time, they placed me on the 11th floor with patients who were more reserved and less disturbed. I was actually more at peace with myself and my surroundings until they decided to transfer me back to the ninth floor for unknown reasons. Maurice was still there. I experienced more fear and anxiety this time and Maurice seemed angrier. When security brought me back to the ninth floor, it was chaotic, noisy and crowded.

I was beyond pissed as I briefly took in the disruptive surroundings. Before I could consider the consequences, I balled up my fist and threw a stiff hammer blow through the narrow glass window that was connected to the security door, which confined us to that floor. I drew back my hand in amazement, saw no blood or cuts from the blast, and felt super human. That short sense of power was quickly suppressed by five large security guards who aggressively bum-rushed me and pushed me toward the seclusion room. The sharp powerful punches to my back and ribs angered me further but the size and strength of these men overwhelmed me. Again, I found myself in a familiar yet undesirable situation of fear, pain, and confinement as large men pound upon me, tearing off the street clothes I wore believing I was being discharged.

Was this to be my eternal cycle of damnation? Every time I thought I was about to be free from that hell hole, it suddenly turned into mocking, pain, fear, rage, isolation… "Oh, God, please forgive me for my lack of faith."

I spent about three days in seclusion and got the same treatment every time I was sent there. When they felt I was calm enough, they put me in a regular room on the floor and I quickly became as gentle as a dove to avoid being thrown back in seclusion. The seclusion rooms were like empty spaces of madness and torment. The dull hot pink hue of the walls and damp sweltering small space was like being in the mouth of a demon, who resided in Western Psych. When the guards put you in there, you don't get out, not even to use the bathroom. I could care less about urinating in the drain on the middle of the floor. But when I had to defecate, most of the time, there weren't any nurses or aides around to hear my cries for the bathroom. So the smell and the heat of that room, day in and day out, became sickening and unbearable.

Maurice looked at me like I was the enemy. I didn't say anything to him as I was led to my room. I was hoping that he forgot about me.

The next morning at breakfast, Maurice sat across from me. When we first met, I had the confidence and attitude of a professional athlete but this time I felt so vulnerable and weak that I sat there in complete silence trying not to make eye contact. I gave a quick glance then dropped my head back down to my plate.

"Yo, what's up, man? You remember me?" Maurice said.

"Yeah, I remember you."

"Yo, why'd you come back?"

"I don't know."

"You all right?"

I couldn't hold back the shame and depression. My eyes filled with tears and streamed down my cheeks. I felt like I let Maurice and others down because I left that place the first time with confidence and peace and returned with shame and humiliation. Maurice surprisingly comforted me and reassured me that I would be fine. I felt like he needed to believe in the existence of God and so did I. That's why I believe he comforted me.

As the days went on, Maurice and I became friends. We stuck together and kept our distance from the other patients... or maybe the other patients just kept their distance from us. I personally didn't want anyone afraid of me. It was counterproductive but Maurice was the type that didn't want to be bothered and since we were friends, I didn't want to cross him. Ironically, he seemed more intimidated by me than I did of him. I began to realize, however, that we had more in common than our physical attributes. Our main commonality was our search for God. Whenever I met others with similar issues and diagnosed with bipolar disorder, I said our "thought lines" were crossing. People like me seemed to be concerned with the same issues, including seeking answers from and through God.

My main concern was the intense fear that consumed me and others like me. Maurice, however, continued to think I was reading his thoughts, which often made it difficult to hold conversations with him. He never accepted my explanation that we studied some of the same material. I stopped talking to him about the Bible so that we could have idle conversations.

One day, Maurice wore a shirt that had the phrase, "Don't ask me 4 shit!" One of the nurse's aides ordered him to change it. I thought that I chose anger over fear, but Maurice kept anger as his best friend.

"Man, I ain't takin' my shirt off for nobody!" he said.

"You take that shirt off or I'm calling security!" the aide told him.

"Call 'em, bitch!" he fired back.

Although his words were a bit harsh, I partly sided with Maurice. We were never allowed to leave the ninth floor and everyone except Maurice and the nurse's aides wore street clothes. After nearly three months, I was tired of wearing and looking at hospital pajamas and slippers so seeing Maurice's shirt let me see a little bit of the outside world, a world I could only experience from my bedroom window nine floors up.

Unfortunately, freedom of speech was not exercised on this floor so Maurice was fighting a losing battle. I knew what was next. They sent the same four guards every time. Before I could warn Maurice, they were there to restrain him. During their restraints, they often threw in a couple of elbows and punches and it pissed me off. I shouted at them in jarring rebellion, but I was in no mood for physical confrontation. So when one of the guards told me to shut up, I did.

Maurice spent a lot of time in seclusion. For me, it was no place for human habitation. I hated seclusion with a passion and the three days I was there were more than enough. I felt sorry for Maurice because I knew what he was going through. All he wanted was relief from his thoughts and answers to his questions. Unfortunately, the doctors, psychiatrists and nurses found Maurice and me unapproachable so the only time we saw them was when we were heavily sedated or in seclusion. Half the time, I couldn't even remember talking to the psychiatrists because I was under the influence of powerful medication.

Maurice was released before me but two weeks later he returned. I asked him why he came back and he said he had gotten into a street fight. Instead of going to jail, the police brought him here. Truthfully, I was kind of glad to see him. But we spoke less and less. When the two largest black men on the floor who stayed angry were together, it created problems. When we were upset at the same time, we were restrained by the guards and sent to seclusion.

Seclusion was the hospital's ultimate weapon against patients, especially Maurice and me. I witnessed excessive force by the guards towards the patients often. There was an incident where the guards restrained an older black woman, who was probably in her late 40s or early 50s. She wanted to go home and was yelling at the staff, demanding that they release her. They called the guards and she became combative. We couldn't understand why it took four large men to restrain a 98-pound older woman? Two guards pressed her head face down on the floor and pulled her arms behind her back. I was outraged but helpless.

"Why do y'all gotta be so rough with her?" I asked.

"You want some, too?" one guard yelled.

I mumbled, "Fuck you!"

Pissed off, I stepped backwards away from the pathetic scene. Maurice, however, wasn't as passive. He threw a barrage of curse words at the guards. When I saw that the guards weren't moving towards him, I rejoined the scene throwing my own set of profanity-laced commentary. Things escalated quickly as our banter caused other patients to berate the guards even more. Finally, five other guards appeared and pushed patients towards their rooms. I didn't fight with any of the guards as they shoved me back in my bedroom door. The guard who seemed to taunt me the most gave me a hard shove through my bedroom door and slammed it shut.

The guards seemed to love bullying us around and there was no use complaining. After all, we were all just a bunch of crazy folk in that place. I was, however, glad that they didn't drag me to seclusion even though I almost incited a riot. I could still hear Maurice's thunderous voice raging on until the guards subdued him. I heard his voice being muffled until there was nothing but silence. I could hear his pain but couldn't do anything to help him. I became so angry that I cried.

Our floor was locked down for about 20 minutes. When the chaos subsided, everyone came out of their rooms except Maurice. I peeked into his room and he wasn't there so I knew he was in seclusion. I stood realizing that the way we were treated wouldn't improve any time soon.

When I was finally being discharged, my mother came to pick me up. Before being released, I had to attend a hearing regarding my follow-up plan. My mother reassured the doctors that I would take the medications and make my regular visits to the doctors and psychiatrists. I held no confidence in my follow-up treatment because of the mistreatment in the hospital. I wanted to say goodbye to Maurice but he was in isolation. I never saw him again.

TERRELLE T. LEWIS

A REVELATION

Accepting Bi-Polar and God's Help

I was discharged to my family the end of the summer. Things were never the same. Everyone seemed to treat me differently and I hated it. I knew they all meant well but their attitudes increased my anxiety. I knew that my demons were not at rest and that another episode was eminent.

Fortunately, my thoughts calmed when I took the large pink pill that the doctors continually forced on me. My only concern was its intolerable side effects that included extreme fatigue. Without the pill, I was full of excitement and energy, but fear followed me constantly. I slowly came to grips that my problem did not lie in my body but in my head.

I returned to the hospital about seven or eight more times after refusing the medication. My final visit, however, I gave in and said to myself, "I'm bipolar."

Over the next several years, doctors and therapists continually reevaluated me and gave me different medications for different reasons. But I leaned more on God by the reading his word. Yes, the Bible became my weapon against fear and anxiety where medication couldn't win.

Earlier in my life, I was faithful to my study of God's word. My only problem was that I didn't believe its authenticity. To me, they were just stories of motivation or maybe just stories. I was about to get a serious wake-up call concerning my spirituality.

No doctor or therapist had ever brought me to this point in my life. They gave pills for voices, for side effects, and for my headaches and many other reasons. But they never gave me the peace that I have now. I always marveled at their reactions when they learned that I never used drugs or alcohol. By their reactions, I assumed that most patients with similar issues must have been drug addicts and alcoholics. All I wanted was for someone to solve my problems and relieve me of this terrible mental burden.

Before I was released from the hospital, my younger sister, Ruth, came to visit me with her husband, Lazarus.

Before then, I only spoke about God with Mrs. Median and I really believed that no one else had a greater understanding of God than she. When Lazarus spoke about God, I couldn't look him in the eyes because I had prejudged him on our first encounter. When he talked about the goodness of Jesus and His unconditional love for me, I slowly raised my eyes and listened intently. He was as reassuring about God as Mrs. Median and he spoke with confidence, quoting scriptures and comparing biblical people to us. He was even able to express what I was dealing with and how I was feeling. He always acknowledged God's presence and protection for me and all who seek Him.

After their visit, I was left with an incredible feeling of zeal that I could hardly contain. For the first time in months, I felt like I had something for which to live.

When I was released, I immediately looked for Lazarus. The more I got to know him, the more confident I became in my spiritual walk. Mrs. Median had been saved for over 30 years and when she talked about Jesus I felt like she was telling me a bedtime story. I listened intently but I only believed in the idea of God, not truly believing in Him and His existence.

When Lazarus spoke to me, it was the first time I heard another person close to my age speak with love and confidence. I felt like I could finally believe. The irony is that Mrs. Median and Lazarus confirmed what I had studied in all my years seeking answers about God.

I had to quickly understand my illness and allow it to work for me, but I didn't how. It was very difficult for me since the symptoms were very unpredictable. With visits to my doctors and psychiatrists and the aide of the large pink pill, I made the effort. Sometimes I felt my struggle was an act of futility even with the large pink pill, known as Depakote which was commonly prescribed to treat anxiety. However, before I could get used to it, they changed my medication. My medications and doctors switched so frequently that I lost confidence in all of them. I was trying hard to get answers to my mental state but no one or nothing could accommodate me. Prozac, Trilafon, Depakote, lithium, Haldol, Clozaril, and many other drugs passed through my blood stream causing extreme fatigue. I hated being sedated because of my experience with the security guards. Almost every altercation with them was when I was partly or fully-sedated, never able to fight back. The medications had me sleeping 10 to 15 hours a night and left me unable to properly function. I felt like my life was being stolen every time I took the pills. I wasn't used to being sleepy all the time or indoors on hot summer days.

I quickly developed a patterned behavior. I became anxious and depressed in the summer and during the holidays. My mood swings kept me from enjoying my family and friends. Inevitably, I became dependent on my medications, but I fought against fatigue and sleeping long hours.

After years of "guinea pig service", doctors introduced me to Seroquel, a medication with minimal side effects. A man my size requires a high dosage. Fortunately, I was able to function a lot better and I was also able to return to my

Bible studies. Reading the Bible became effortless when I searched wholeheartedly for God's wisdom. In fact, the more I read, the more God opened my understanding. I began to defeat my anxiety and fears.

Finding a Mentor

As the years went by, Lazarus and I became like blood brothers. We went to church, studied the Bible, and prayed together. He spoke to me about my fears and insecurities and continually professed that God had not forsaken me. He even encouraged me to use the other God-given talents I had such as poetry, creative writing and others. Any time I was afraid, I called him.

The difference between Lazarus and Mrs. Median was that she spoke from a motherly perspective while Lazarus spoke from a young man's perspective. I listened to both but Lazarus was able to discuss many of my issues from a man's point of view. Lazarus often told me that I reminded him of himself when he was my age. He was only about five years older, but he spoke with knowledge and wisdom beyond his years.

I learned later that Lazarus had preached before and that he desired to become a minister. What really amazed me was how he convinced me to live my life without guilt or fear and to seek God through his word. To me, that was unheard of. I thought that my manhood would always interfere with my spirituality and that I could never break through that barrier between Jesus Christ and me. But I read in Proverbs where it says, *"Acknowledge me in all your ways and I will direct your path."* This scripture along with many others came back to my memory and impacted my life. My mind found rest from racing thoughts.

I re-entered Bible studies with confidence and courage and thus began a new walk with God. I would never say that I lived happily ever after because real life is not that simple. But I did begin to focus on my spiritual walk as well as my natural. Could they be one in the same?

I still talked to Mrs. Median from time to time but I listened with greater enthusiasm. I no longer felt like an outsider when she talked about the Bible and I finally felt like God had a plan for my life. I used to rage on not knowing who or what I wanted to be. I really didn't have a role model.

Although I loved my dad, he was not the man I wanted to become. As I said before, my parents' lives seemed to contradict everything that I thought Godly people were to represent. I believe that played a major role in my misplaced anger and my identity issues in Christ.

I don't fully blame my parents. I now have a testimony because God revealed Himself to me and I allow his spirit to work and guide me. In fact, the more I read the Bible, the more I got to know Him. His word changed the boy inside of me and matured me to a man. The anger, however, remained, but I concluded that I'd rather be angry than afraid. The aggressive vigor of anger gave me strength to battle my demons.

Now I live in a way that demons fear me, or should I say the God in me.

Lazarus continued to coach me years later. He put together a team of workers that included Ruth, Vashti, and me. In this brief time, Lazarus utilized each of our talents and encouraged us to do great things in the process. We learned a lot about ourselves and each other and I became a different person. I never backed down from any tasks that

Lazarus asked of me. He yelled a lot and cursed at us while doing it in love. His influence on us was so powerful that we thought we couldn't do anything without him. In fact, much of what he taught us was from a "street perspective", yet some of its effects allowed no room for fear. I truly loved that but when I was overcome with anger, I forgot how to calm myself down.

Getting a Life-Changing Revelation

During this stage of my life, I had fallen in love with an older woman. I also stopped taking my full, prescribed dosage of medication. I got so frustrated that even Lazarus could no longer mend my anger problem and consequently landed me another visit to the psychiatric hospital. This time had nothing to do with fear, but my uncontrollable rage after breaking up with my girlfriend.

When I was released, I had a revelation that catapulted me into a full-blown positive lifestyle; I realized that I was too dependent on Lazarus and lost sight of my spiritual walk with God. I believed that God wanted me to be more depended upon Him.

Our team lasted about four years. I still talk with Lazarus from time to time, but I realized that our experience with him was only for a season. The knowledge that we attained helped us become "go getters", and I know the Holy Spirit influenced much of Lazarus's actions.

Vashti developed into a busy and upstanding woman, a contrast to the person she was years earlier.

Ruth and Lazarus separated but remained friends. I am still working and seeking the Lord without fear and I continue to develop and use the gifts that God gave me. As for my anger, I am able to keep it in its proper perspective along with the help of medication.

My brother Enoch got married to a beautiful woman named, Priscilla, who is a very wise, intelligent, and God-fearing woman. My hope is that Enoch may find his confidence in God and realize that He is with him and loves him, too. I'm not saying that he doesn't believe in God, but I do believe that our faith in God was similar because of our childhood experiences.

A Woman's Impact

I allowed my anger and jealousy over an older woman to get the best of me. I learned a lot from that experience and I'm much wiser for it. She indirectly helped me to see past our physical attraction and observe her intentions along with mine.

I won't say her name but I will summarize our relationship through this poem:

The Smile of a Tease...

A constant wink in her eye and blew kisses through the breeze.

Came the invitation and the call, through the smile of a tease.

I fell rapidly in love, but the love came too fast.

As she wondered about our future, I focused on our past.

Her demeanor was mom and wife, even though I did not ask.

In return I kept my word, and raked every leaf from her grass.

A family so large and diverse like a secret ingredient in a mixture.

Yet I wondered why she sighed when she sorted through family pictures.

She lived a life before I saw black people fighting for equal rights.

And reassured it did not matter that I am black and she is white.

Our intimacy was so intense like we'd never meet eyes again.

And loved the moments in love until she gave ear to her friends.

I wrote poetry about her and pampered her with kisses.

To the point of lifting burdens and offering to do the dishes.

But as life moved on, our relationship transformed.

As my anger turned to rage, while a new thought was born.

But fate took its turn of the page she read was absurd.

Apparently I insulted her without ever saying a word.

She took the words that I wrote out of context and frame.

By my words that I expressed queried her faith toward her name.

None of my words could mend her heart after that event.

For the climbing of our love took a quick, drastic descent.

My anger was kindled as we began to drift apart.

What hurt all the more was that she toyed with my heart.

She chose wisdom over lust rejecting our relationship.

And at our last supper we shared silence, after that, I paid the tip.

I turned to her, expressionless, and gave her my final kiss.

Getting up from the table before any were dismissed.

I no longer hear her voice which sounded through the breeze.

My thoughts of her are gone, even the smile of her tease.

This woman had a profound effect on every other relationship I had thereafter. And though we separated on odd terms, I hold no ill feelings towards her. Since then, I've been with different women, but it was difficult to be open to any long-lasting relationship. I focused on developing my talents and the word of God. Yes, I had distractions. I've come to the conclusion that everybody has problems and issues. I knew that accepting the spirit of God in your life meant to accept that He is fully capable of sorting out all your problems and all your issues.

If you think that your relationship with God has to be public, you may want to reconsider. Your love for God will be apparent from your actions. If you want to know who truly loves God, *"You will know them by their fruits."* Just remember, nobody's perfect. Nobody!

I used to think that wisdom came through relationships. I was partly correct but I also believe that it depends on what type of relationship you're in that gives you wisdom. A woman companion always found her way into my life. Many times, I thought of the women that I had been with and bookmarked my intimate moments with them. But there is much more to a relationship than sex. Before now, my longest relationship lasted about nine months and sex was the defining attribute in it.

I still loved the presence of a woman, especially one that I was attracted to. The problem was in the baggage that women carried when leaving one relationship and entering another. Some have emotional scars and when they meet a gentle man by nature like me, they seemed to buck against that part of me. They inevitably try to bring out the side of the man they once knew from their past. Many of the women from my past expected violence or verbal abuse and received nothing but love and concern. Consequently, they were not familiar with that type of love and unconsciously sought out what they had become accustomed to. When I was unable to oblige, they left and that became my emotional scar in almost all of my brief relationships. Now I'm not saying that I was perfect either. Lord knows I had my issues as well, but I was never in a relationship where I mentally or physically abused a woman. I guess somehow I thought I could 'save' these women. Maybe that's why I unconsciously sought after women with emotional scars. That's why I remained single for so long.

I also have become aware of who I am as an individual, learning my dislikes, desires, and needs. I like who I am. More importantly, I have and continue to get closer to God.

Finding Comfort in God

Soon, I felt God's comforting spirit and the undeniable mercy He had on my life so much that I started depending more on His word more than on doctors and medication. That's not to say I gave up medication and treatments. I still speak with psychiatrists and take my medication. But because I learned that God is in in control of my life, I no longer grudgingly take medication and talk with psychiatrists. I now tell them how God influences my life and how productive I've become. Most of the doctors and psychiatrists would rather credit the medication for my healing but I know better. The meds help but who gave man the knowledge to create them?

I am no longer afraid to read God's word or seek his understanding and wisdom like when I used fear as an excuse to sin. I have read that, *"My people perish for lack of knowledge."*

Another verse that has stuck with me is, *"Wisdom is the principle thing, therefore get wisdom, and with all your getting, get understanding!"* Now I realize that to understand the purpose God has for me and all who seek Him, we must repent and turn away from rebellious knowledge, habits, and ways that defy God.

Is this even possible? It seems that everything we do is sin. Can't do this. Can't do that. Can't say this. Can't say that. What can we do? I know it sounded like I have a lot of resentment towards seeking God, and for a while I did. However, as I stopped looking at my life as a victim, I began taking baby steps toward God while turning away from sin. It's hasn't been as difficult as I thought. I'm not saying that rejecting temptation is easy every time, but when you realize that God is with you and in you, denying sin is a little easier and brings you closer to God. I can't forget to tell you that my return to church was like the Prodigal Son. When I was going through my mental breakdown, I stopped going to church for a long time. But when I realized, or better yet accepted, that the Holy Spirit was within me, I was ready to learn and reconnect with a people and a preacher that could guide and connect with me. To listen to a Bible believing, faith-based, Jesus Christ-teaching church, was and is still a major part of my growth.

The Book of Ephesians taught me how to wear the armor of God and face the onslaught. I became better equipped in faith and in courage. I believe my lack of wisdom and understanding contributed to my past episodes which became stepping stones. The more I read the Bible with the intent of believing in the integrity of God's word, the more I know Him intimately. No pill has healed me of my so-called mental disorder. No doctor has told me about the love of God. I believe that my desire to do His will has changed the way I think. Knowing the will of God for my life has given me faith, strength and hope against this cold, evil world and by the Holy Spirit of Jesus Christ I am guided daily from apathy to greatness.

I have no regrets going to God. Every day I wake up, I experience joy, love, and peace, I feel confident in the new day that God will reveal a new thing to me and I will give Him the glory He deserves.

I discovered in the book of Romans that nothing or no one can separate me from the love of God.

SURVIVING SETON HOUSE

Moving on, I saw my walk of faith increase. I had been dependent on monthly disability checks and public assistance. When I was diagnosed with bipolar disorder, I tried to live without medical assistance and psychiatric treatment. After discontinuing my meds without my doctor's consent, I was confident for a while. I felt my strength return and my senses magnified. I felt so good. In fact, I might have felt a little too good. It wasn't until later that I heard the word manic. "You seem a little manic," they said. When I asked the meaning of the word, I said to myself, "I shall never again be otherwise!" I loved being manic, having all my senses magnified and feeling unstoppable, but a man's mind can only take so much. I had run from the diagnosis of manic depression bipolar disorder, but eventually accepted it.

I made a decision to finally submit to my meds. I no longer felt a need for spiritual growth or a need for therapeutic sessions with people who were not dealing with life from a black man's perspective. I remember when a doctor's analysis caused social workers to discontinue my monthly disability checks. I was angry and felt entitled to the money. I called Mrs. Median and expressed my distress to her.

"Mrs. Median, they stopped my SSI checks. Can you believe that?!?"

I wasn't prepared for her answer.

"Good! Get a job and go to work!" she said.

I was used to receiving a soft, gentle answer from her. But on this day, she gave me a harsh cold answer to help me "grow up." But it was also endearing and the truth.

At first, going back to full-time work was not easy, but it kept my mind occupied. I was content and consistent. As long as I had my medication, my psychiatric treatments, and my family and friends' support, I worked harder and longer at each job. I continued to further my education so that I could find a career that encompassed my gift to draw. I applied for a job in the Crafton area of Pittsburgh and found that they starred black applications to avoid our presence within their company. I had a Caucasian friend from my trade school who also applied for the same job. After she was hired, she befriended a member of the human resources department. One day, as they were having idle conversation, my friend noticed my name on a stack of applications. She asked the woman if the star on the top of the application meant that they intended to hire me. The HR rep said, "No. Stars are to alert the HR department of black applications. Do you know him?"

My friend replied, "No, I was just wondering about the star."

"We won't hire him." the HR rep said.

This young white female from Connecticut could not believe the racism that she had just witnessed in Southwestern Pennsylvania in 2002. She looked around and realized there were no blacks working there.

As she told me the story, she cried. The debates we used to have at school about job equality ended. In fact, we both applied for that job as a result of one of our debates. After about a week, she left the job and Pittsburgh and moved back to Connecticut.

I continued to seek employment with no success until the school finally sent me to a job in Trafford, PA. I was hired as a freelance artist and was promised a full-time position. But that never happened. Friends spotted the job announcement in the local newspaper and I realized they weren't going to hire me after all. It was a dagger in my back and my boss was always unavailable when I tried to ask about it. I decided that paying my bills outweighed my desire to work in my field of choice.

Frustrated, I filled out applications and resumes that had nothing to do with art. I found myself yielding to the field of security.

I felt good and a sense of purpose in protecting people and their assets. I worked in schools, for commercial clients, and secured high profile people and buildings in Pittsburgh and Washington, D.C.

My brother invited me to come to D.C. He moved there after graduating Temple University and found his wife there a short time later. He saw my progress and felt my pain in needing to leave home. I, however, left home with a certain amount of relief as well as an equal amount of guilt. My mother took care of me all my life and now that I was mentally strong enough to go, she would be alone. I was the last to "leave the nest" and didn't want to leave her in the rundown, crime-filled area in which we lived the previous 12 years. I knew God would keep her, but I had trouble letting her go as much as she did me.

The first month with my brother was as expected. We were tighter than we had ever been and I felt as excited as a college student on the first semester away from home, just like when I followed him to Temple University in Philadelphia. The second month was a bit complicated because I had to find an HMO program to accommodate my psychiatric treatments. When I finally found one, the doctor felt I no longer needed Clozaril, which affects a person's white blood cell count. In my case, it nearly depleted them. He prescribed another medication at a very low dosage. I immediately felt the effects of the change. I was on a relatively high dosage of Clozaril, and though my white blood cells returned to their normal count, my mental stability began to waver. Withdrawal from the medication changed my mood. My confidence slowly diminished and no matter how many times I expressed my concerns to the doctor, he arrogantly dismissed me. My brother got agitated at the doctor's decisions but he watched closely and kept records of my declining behavior.

I could no longer keep a grip on "reality" and one day I slipped into another psychotic episode. I felt hopeless. My surroundings appeared a pale hue of green. My heart raced as if someone was after me. I couldn't hear anything except a high-pitched ringing, like the flat-line sound from a heart monitor. I tried not to panic since I knew what was happening. I used the little faith I had to keep me from doing anything rash, like suicide. The thoughts of eternal damnation, extreme heat, torment, and extreme pain kept me from committing suicide. That day was my lowest state of consciousness. I never experienced anything like it and expect I never will again.

Seton House

I did have another episode, which was my final breakdown. It led me to a hospital in Washington, D.C., called Seton House, where God gave me my revelation.

My sister in-law got home just as I was considering wandering off. She saw my strange behavior, called my brother, and rushed me to the nearest mental institution. When we arrived, I perceived that I was now in a holding place awaiting final judgment. I listened to the security guards at the door speaking to one another saying, "It's about that time! Yes sir. We about to be outta here!" I heard another guard ask, "Is he coming after you?" as he looked in my direction.

"Who me?" I asked.

The guard behind me answered, "Nah bra. I'm here all night. He's comin' for you he ha ha!" My heart pounded as I wondered who this person was and who he was planning to take, and where? I sat next to my sister in-law and cried. She comforted me, taking my head into her arm and rubbing my forehead. As I listened to the security guards' idle conversation, I perceived that this person or demonic escort that they were speaking about was coming for me. I stood up and decided to break through the large metal door where the guards stood. I kept hearing them say things like, "He'll be here any minute." I looked at the clock high on the wall behind me and it said 3:10. 3:15? Wasn't that the witching hour in The Amityville Horror when the guy awoke to kill his family? That was 3:15 a.m. though, wasn't it? I was feeling mentally unstable, just as I did when I was taken to Western Psyche the day I walked mindlessly on the parkway.

That day, time seemed to stand still and fly at the same time, if you can imagine that. So whoever was coming to escort me to hell or put me in eternal chains was about to come through that door when that clock reached 3:15. I looked one last time at my sister in-law, who looked worried. My eyes widened and my muscles tensed. I looked at the clock; both hands pointed directly at the three. Here we go!

"Terrelle?" a voice said with a faint accent.

I quickly jerked my head to the voice.

"Are you Terrelle Lewis?"

"Yeah."

I saw a shorter Asian man wearing glasses, tight khakis and a cheap pale green button down shirt and olive green and gray striped tie. He asked me to come into an empty room with my sister-in-law, but I wanted to see who was about to come through that door and get me. He took me by the arm. I refused to take my eyes off the door. As he spoke softly, he grabbed me tighter. Had I not felt my sister in-law's soft touch and heard her sweet voice, I might have had another violent outbreak.

I looked at her and was less agitated. Although I wanted to watch the door a little longer, I relaxed my muscles and grudgingly walked in. Right after the nurse's aide closed the door, I heard a lot of commotion on the other side. The Asian guy asked me the usual obligatory questions but I was more focused on the commotion outside. My sister in-law answered the man for me until I threw in a few yeses and nos. After he finished, I quickly moved toward the door.

"Terrelle, wait!" he said.

I had already twisted the doorknob and swung the door open. I quickly looked to my right where I could see the metal door. There was only the guard sitting by the door.

"I guess he took all of 'em," I thought. I later realized that it was a shift change and some of the guards left.

I stayed there overnight and then was transferred to Seton House, where the hallucinations were abundant, auditory and visual my first night. I was so angry with the doctor for not listening to me, or considering my brother's concerns. I thought I was going to live a normal life with a decent paying job and a happy social life with a girlfriend that provided me casual sex. But that wasn't part of God's plan for my life at the time.

The patients were as odd as I had expected but none seemed more distant from any psychological treatment than me... and one other patient. She was an elderly woman who wore a long night gown with short sleeves. There were times when I thought she wasn't there but I remember her reciting scriptures and lines from gospel songs. I always had a phobia of elderly women from my childhood, especially my paternal great grandmother. This woman reminded me of her except her hair was longer and whiter. Sometimes I looked at her as some type of angel.

One day, I approached her and asked her who she was. She looked up at me with her pale grayish-brown eyes that seemed to have little life in them and continued reciting scripture. Her fallen countenance bothered me so I raised my hand slowly to express compassion and respect but she blocked my hand. I reached up again with my other hand and she blocked that too. She continued to speak in her low voice while reciting scripture. I suddenly felt anxious and walked around her to the other side of the room, never taking my eyes off her. We stared at each other. She continued to speak and I remained silent. I really couldn't hear what she was saying, but I know it was the same repetitive words from the Bible. What bothered me even more was her relentless, focused, expressionless, stare. It got to the point where I didn't notice any of the other patients or nurses in the room. I tried to hear what she was saying. It sounded like "I hope. I hope. I hope." Her voice was raspy and deep. After that, I tried to stay away from her, but somehow she always caught my eye. I tried not to engage or even pass her. When I did, all I heard was, "I hope... I hope... I hope." She always caught me staring at her.

I constantly looked to see where she was during medicine distribution, at breakfast, and before we went to our rooms at the end of the night. The more I saw her, the more I feared her. She looked so much like my great grandmother whom I had nightmares about as a child. I felt like that helpless child who could not escape the long, thin, dark outstretched fingers of a frizzy, gray-haired, hunchback black witch. That's how I saw my great grandmother when I was four and that's how I saw this old woman.

One night right before bedtime, I sat across the room to ensure that she went to her bedroom. I thought I heard her walking around the night before repeating, "I hope... I hope... I hope." As I watched a nurse escort her into her room, she was still saying the same thing. Just before I breathed a sigh of relief, she quickly turned, hunched over and said, "I hope you die! Hahahahaha!"

Her last words and nightmarish cackle kept me up all night. It caused me to become a lighter sleeper.

It was hard to sleep in mental institutions when your mind is full of confusion and tormented with fear and guilt 24-7. I lay my head on their uncomfortable pillows and slid under their scratchy, thin, wool knitted blankets. I also had to keep one eye open on my chemically-imbalanced roommate.

Seton House had a lot of strange patients and some things I experienced had me thinking again that I must be the anti-Christ. I remember the fall of Lucifer as described in the book of Ezekiel. The story always haunted me because I thought that if I could not attain the peace of Jesus Christ's Holy Spirit, then I must be destined to play out the revelation of the abomination. I wanted to receive the Holy Spirit and at one point the doctors and nurses put me in seclusion because they feared my rebellion. No one seemed to understand my thoughts or the spiritual warfare I faced. I took any and all medications they offered, hoping that one would take effect and bring me some peace of mind so that I could fall asleep. None worked. I sat on the edge of the bed inside the seclusion room refusing food and drink. I stared outside the dirty caged window listening to faint sounds. I set my mind upon tarrying until the Holy Spirit fell upon me and the light of heaven shined down with me speaking in other tongues but it did not happen on that night or any other night.

My dreams became my consciousness as I walked about the room acting them out. They were always about the Medians and my family members, especially my brother who would come to visit me. Sometimes I didn't know if I was asleep or awake. All I knew was that I had no peace, no escape from racing thoughts, and no satisfaction of a lovely slumber. I constantly worried about those I cared about. I lost track of days and time as usual and the strangest of things plagued me there, such as constantly seeing Mrs. Median seated in a chair with a look of disgust on her face or Mr. Median coming later to avenge his wife's death which was caused by her prayers for me. These were the types of things I was dealing with.

I highly respected Mr. Median and his family. After all, they treated me as their own and kept me on the straight and narrow. Now, he found me at Seton House, mentally vulnerable and seeking my life. He and Ruach often sat next to me and I was very aware of his presence and his touch but he never spoke to me. Ruach became my roommate for most of my stay there and I had no idea why. He had no history of mental health issues, nor did his dad. So what the heck were they doing here in Seton House? Were they working undercover as volunteers so that they could get close enough to kill me? The weight of my guilt and the burden of my mental distress were too much to bare. But seeing how everything played out kept me going. I wasn't sure if Mr. Median and Ruach were really there but I continued to hear them. The voices were undeniably theirs. I was content that there were two among us that were familiar to me, but disturbed by their intentions.

I convinced myself that my lack of faith and destructive behavior somehow destroyed Mrs. Median. I thought that her prayers were intercepted by some type of demonic legion and that they tracked her down and claimed her immortal soul. It had to be the reason Mr. Median was there. He came to sever the line of doubt that spouted from me and stop me from administering the tribulation against the people who were left behind. I was once again feeling that the rapture had taken place and that the real terror was about to begin.

The next day around lunchtime, I was in line at the med window waiting to receive my daily dosage. I can't remember what they were giving me at that point since I received anything they thought might work. I usually just threw down whatever pill they gave me before they could explain what it was. On this particular day, the old lady stood near me in line. She looked more content, yet a bit somber as she sang an old Negro spiritual. I was angry about what she did the night before so her songs agitated me. I cut in front of her to get my pills, hoping to start some static. She looked up at me as I received my pills. I looked down at her as I brushed past her shoulder. I was waiting to see if she was going to expose that dark, hunchback witch that she had revealed to me before. She didn't. She walked and got her medication. She placed the cup from the water she washed her pill down with back on the ledge of the med window and slowly walked away. She continued to sing that depressing, yet humbling old gospel song.

I felt an old conviction of wanting to submit to God's Holy Spirit, but I didn't know how to receive it. I continued watching her walk towards a hallway. I jumped up, not wanting to lose her around the corner. As I frantically walked across the room, I maneuvered around other patients, shoving some out my way. I finally reached the hallway and there she stood under a light that made her appear horrifying. She looked like the witch from the night before but was still singing that song.

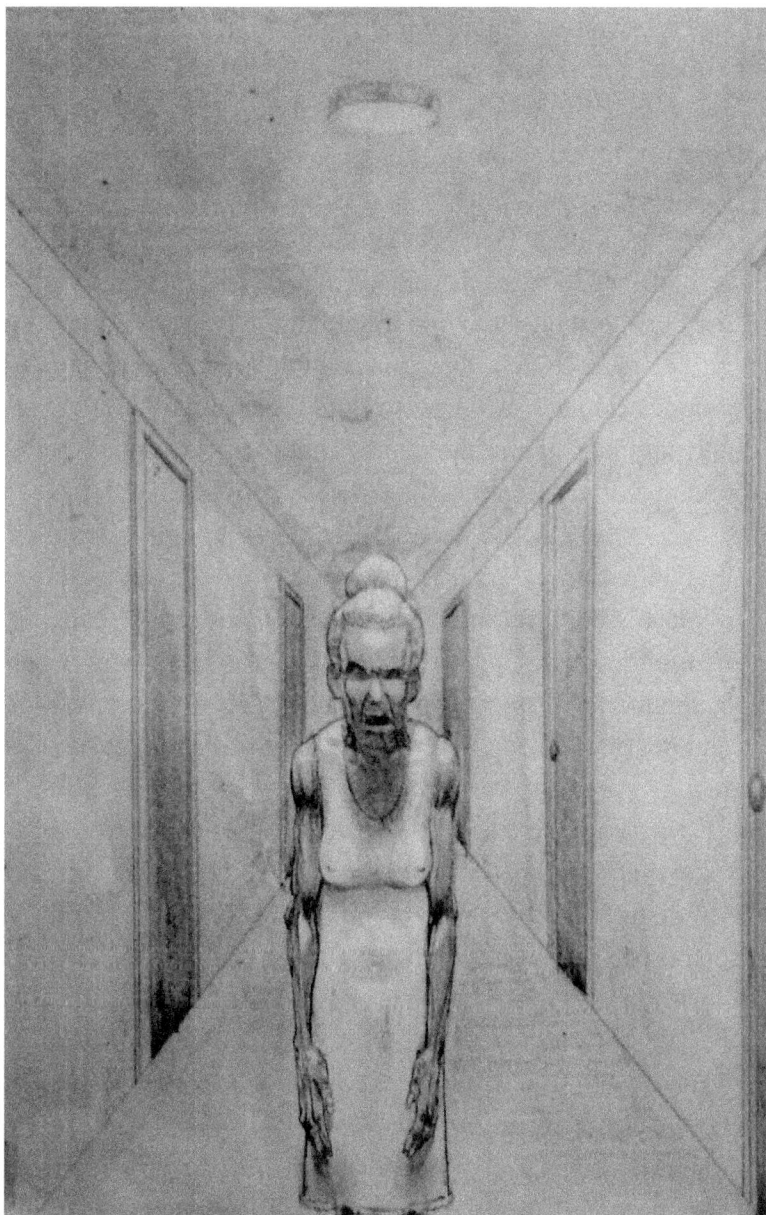

Her shadowy figure enraged me. To my own surprise, I walked up to her, grabbed her by her neck and angrily asked, "You wanna go to heaven?" I dragged her backwards down the hallway. Without struggling, she placed her hands on mine and closed her eyes as if she was prepared to die. Her courage shamed me. I loosened my grip, dropped her, and whispered, "I'll go first!" I ran down the corridor and dove into a hole that would take me to the other side. To my dismay, I actually slammed into the wooden doors of a linen closet and bruised my head, neck and shoulders. I was still alive. That was the most desperate and unpredictable thing that I can ever remember doing.

The next day, I entered the men's room and pushed my face into defecated waters. I facetiously put my head inside a plastic hamper and shut the lid hoping to escape my mental torment. But it was pointless and a bit painful, not to mention that suicide was still no option for me. I was lost and angry and I felt that if I was the Anti-Christ, then so be it.

These are the last days and many signs that were spoken of in the Book of Revelation have taken place. The fact that I thought I knew when the rapture would take place was preposterous. Yet my thoughts were consistent with biblical occurrences, at least as I interpreted them.

Two scriptures kept me from overthinking my situation: Matthew 24:36, *"But of that day and hour knoweth no man, no, not the angels of heaven, but my Father only"* and Proverbs 3:5, *"Trust in the Lord with all thine heart and lean not unto thine own understanding."* Ironically, what I thought was my mental disposition at that time was slowly becoming my source of reference.

I continued to battle the many dreams and visions that kept me awake, yet their intensity and content were intoxicating. I looked forward to the night even though I couldn't sleep. My family and friends became a part of a movie-like vision with dark-themed music. Seeing them night after night pushed me to complete this ongoing story in my head of my family origins in a dark world. Sounds like the title of a book or movie doesn't it? But these visions were real and every night around the same time, the dream started from my window at Seton House.

An intense drum beat played and I looked out over the silhouetted shoulder of my brother and first cousin, Caleb. I spied the darkness until my eyes caught a single street light. I was levitated to it and I witnessed someone being shot. I never knew the perpetrators or the victim. Something or someone always blocked my view right before I could clearly see the vision. I heard the rising sounds and scourges of people in stadium-like surroundings, and all I wanted to know was, "Who in this entire stadium of people, famous or not, could tell me what I needed to heal me, or figure out what's wrong with my mind?" I looked to famous actors like Morgan Freeman, Larry Fishburne, and Denzel Washington. Surely these famous, profound, black men could help get my thoughts focused so I could be famous and content like them. That's what I was seeking.

When I was moved toward them to engage their words of wisdom, Larry Fishburne was filled with rage, Denzel Washington was filled with apprehension, and Morgan Freeman was full of... yeah that! I still have not met any of these men. But I felt like no one could help me. I lost hope in all doctors, medication, and all opinions of so-called successful people. I no longer wanted to be famous; I just wanted to be free of my thoughts, free of me.

One night when the darkness seemed infinite, I began to fall asleep. I was exhausted and my body was weak. When I closed my eyes, I felt my body rise as though I was levitating. What I saw was neither a vision nor dream; it looked like a dark tunnel with a pale green light illuminating the way. The wire-lined walls and pipes looked like I was traveling down a sewage pipe. I started moving slowly but then I accelerated. I heard a voice inside say, "Repent!" It was what I was searching for.

I heard the word shoot from my mouth like a great megaphone and my trip down this tunnel came to an abrupt stop. My body slowly descended back upon the bed. I slept peacefully until the sun shined through the window the next morning.

I wish I could tell you that I was perfectly fine from that point on; I wasn't. However, the word 'repent' became the foundation for which I would build.

To repent is to acknowledge sorrow to God of an unworthy act, such as sin. It also is the act of turning away from and discontinuing the habits of sin. Mrs. Median had explained that word to me over and over again but I couldn't comprehend it. Truthfully, I wasn't ready. I wasn't ready to submit to a strict life of obedience and sacrifice, which included giving my wants and needs to God. I still had things to do. I had to find a wife, a job, and my own home. I had no idea how God could cater to my desires especially when He was so angry with me. I thought, "If He wasn't, I wouldn't be sitting here in this stupid hospital gown and dirty slippers, talking to myself with a bunch of crazy ass folk in Seton House."

I knew I was angry with God but was never willing to admit it. I still found myself in the seclusion rooms arguing back and forth with the old black woman who was now a complete nightmare against me. Apparently when I didn't kill her in the hallway, she sought to stress me out until I would take my own life. I heard her in the other room yelling and bantering. I was trying to ignore her but she was relentless. When she could no longer torment me, she went after Mr. Median and Ruach. She had become the witch that I first took her for. She spoke in Mrs. Median's voice and lured Mr. Median and Ruach into the room with her. She said, "It was Terrelle's doubt that killed me." When I heard that, I was livid but unable to defend myself against her illusion. She told them that I was in the next room. I had no place to run, no place to hide. I crawled under the bed. Mr. Median and Ruach came in and Mr. Median spoke in his deep angry voice, "You should've believed, boy!" They stood over me as tears streamed down my face, "I'm sorry! I'm sorry!" I cried out. They raised their feet to stomp me and the first blow awakened me. I was on the floor in an empty room. I could still hear Mr. Median and Ruach. They were stomping on the witch in the next room. I could hear her laughing as they pummeled her. She tricked them! She was ready to die so she used her black magic to trick them into killing her. I should've been the one being stomped. It was my fault that Mrs. Median died.

"Mr, Median, don't!" I yelled.

It was too late. I heard the sound of bodies dropping to the floor like weights, and the voices continued as cries fell through the floor screaming, "Noooo…!"

I was horrified. Mr. Median and Ruach broke the commandment, "Thou shalt not kill!" They were gone!

Suddenly, two men came in the room and lifted me off the floor. They carried me out of the seclusion area and back to a different room where they shoved me in like it was a jail cell and shut the door behind me. I couldn't believe my eyes. Ruach was sitting in the dark on one of the beds, wearing a black shirt and red shorts. He sat quietly with his hands folded and a poker face.

"Ruach what's going on?" I said.

He didn't respond. I was afraid to leave him so I quietly sat on the other bed and kept my distance. We were both quiet until the entire floor was quiet. Ruach stood up, cracked open the door and peeked out. He was looking for his dad. I didn't want him to leave me. I jumped up too.

Mr. Median left Seton House a few times and returned telling Ruach to stay behind. I assumed he told him to keep an eye on me. I didn't know where he went, but each time he returned, he was focused on stopping my Anti-Christ blasphemy or saving his son and others from me. I also noticed that each time he returned, his hair and beard had more gray in it.

On this night, after Ruach peeked out the room, he went back to his bed and grabbed what appeared to be a small duffel bag. I followed closely behind him. As I peeked out over his head, I saw Mr. Median seated on a long bed. His face was dim but full of wisdom. His hair and beard were white like wool and he was the size of a 20-foot man. I perceived that he had gone to heaven to ask God for forgiveness. I assumed that he came back for Ruach. I felt that if any man had this profound privilege, it would be him. I noticed a bright light from an open space that stretched from one end of the wall to the other in front of Mr. Median's bed. Ruach ran to his dad, seemingly unaware of the bright space, but I saw it and apparently Mr. Median could to. As he sat up from his bed, he moved in slow motion. He stretched forth his hand to stop Ruach from coming closer. I pulled my head back into the room. I didn't want to see what would happen next. There was silence. When I looked again, they were gone.

The next day, I awoke to an empty room. I had already felt the isolation of the patients but now the doctors and nurse's aides were just as distant. No one could reason with me or understand why I couldn't sleep or interact with the others. I had no one to turn to. No one understood what I was dealing with except Mr. Median and Ruach. When I got up for breakfast, I saw a man in a black shirt and red shorts already eating. His back was to me. Was it Ruach? I thought maybe he hadn't been granted entrance in God's kingdom. He was condemned to this sad, depressing, horrid place with all the other patients. When I walked over to the man, I discovered that it was an older gentlemen with a thick black mustache, a low, even haircut and sorrowful eyes. This place was my hell and I felt like I was never going to leave the relentless, painful, torment of Seton House.

For the rest of my time there, I didn't speak to anyone. I was condemned to my thoughts and felt the burden of destiny. My brother came one more time with Vashti. She had never seen me in any of the mental institutions. I sat weary and sedated in the activity room where they had visitation time. When she saw me, she gently wrapped her arms around my neck and shoulders, kissed me on the cheek and walked out of the room trying to hide her tears. My brother told me that I was to be released from Seton House the next day. I asked him the date and was relieved when he said only a month had past.

I dropped the weight of my delusion like a ton of bricks. I concluded that Mrs. Median and Mr. Median were still alive and that the man wearing the black shirt and red shorts was merely another patient. This long traumatic chapter of Seton House was now ready to be left behind. But there was no way I would forget it.

When my brother came for me the next day, I was already packed and sitting in the activity room. He walked in and helped me to my feet. I took one last look at the gentleman in the black shirt and red shorts, who was sitting at a small table by himself. He looked up at me with a face full of pain and sorrow. I felt like I was abandoning my best friend and as I stared, my brother took my arm and asked, "You okay?" I didn't answer but dropped a tear of compassion while keeping my eyes on the man. When I walked out the front door, I got into my brother's truck, leaned my head on the inside of the door window and said goodbye to Seton House.

Leaving Seton House

As we reached the downtown area of the Washington, D.C., I looked out the window and thought I saw a patient whom I encountered at Western Psyche, another from Charter Fairmount, and yet another from my hometown in Wilkinsburg. I really wasn't concerned about any auditory or visual hallucinations. I was looking for the end of the world, God-like wrath, or persecution of Christians-type stuff. But I saw nothing, well nothing that was outwardly apparent.

I closed my eyes to rest and before I knew it, we were parking. The burden of re-entering a routine life was too much for me. I didn't want to get out of the truck but I grudgingly did. Enoch and Vashti carried my things to the house and as my brother fumbled for his keys at the front door, he made a comment that he was experiencing déjà vu. Coincidently, so was I.

Enoch said he had to go to the store and asked if we wanted to go with him. I prayed that Vashti would say yes because I already had my answer. She and my brother reluctantly left me in the sweet quietness of his living room. I looked over at the phone thinking of my friends, so I called Mrs. Median. When she answered, I asked if she was okay and if she had recently visited Washington, D.C. She said no. She gave a reassuring chuckle knowing my issues. As we talked, I told her that I had just got out of the hospital. She said she had already heard and said that she kept me in her prayers. We talked until I was confident that everything and everyone were back to normal. I felt more awake after we talked.

I sat down and turned on the television. The first image that appeared was a commercial showing a beautiful woman wearing next to nothing. I had already struggled with pornographic addiction. Before my experience at Seton House, I thought my life could be comfortably lived in my private life of pornographic gratification. What harm could it do to anyone? What harm could it do to me? I couldn't possibly catch any sexually transmitted diseases or be burdened with a complicated relationship. Gorgeous women were the loves of my life. I could make love to them as often as I desired, whenever I desired. But the guilt of this addiction was constantly against me. God knows our thoughts and I believed that it was his Holy Spirit that shouted, "Repent!" to and through me.

I went upstairs to the guest room, opened up the closet door and reached into a box that had about eight pornographic movies. I carried them down the steps, outside and dropped them into the empty trash can in front of the house. I shut the door and sat back on the futon. I gave God a praise of thanks and sat quietly in the living room until my brother and sister returned.

I made a decision to return to Pittsburgh to reestablish my friendship with my brother-in-law. I called him a week before my decision and our conversation about God ignited the drive that I have no intention of ending.

THE JOURNEY
TAKES A TURN

When I embarked on this life-changing quest with Lazarus as my guide, my whole character and personality changed. At that time, I thought anger was my only weapon against the fear that haunted me. But fear was joined by depression and they both tried to consume me. I defended my brother in-law's name consistently for the four years I followed him. I believed he was a strong man of God and I still do. But during that journey, Lazarus took me to a deeper perspective in my spiritual walk and like a father taking the training wheels off a child's bike and letting go, I went forward without fear.

First, I had to deal with the aggressive and defensive personality I developed.

My loyalty to Lazarus was undeniable and no one could convince me to question his loyalty to God, not even my brother or mother. My sisters were partners in this journey as well so I showed loyalty to them, too. I was focused.

I finally understood the true meaning of true repentance. Lazarus' demeanor was fearless and relentless to the point that even my dreams concerning him increased my defense for him. He had an incredible gift for breaking down barriers and revealing lies and misconduct in people's lives. He seemed so driven by God's power. It was futile to turn a deaf ear to him and even harder to be independent of his unique "coaching style".

I learned a wealth of self-sustaining morals and values from Lazarus. I still use them. But it wasn't until my mid-30s that I finally became aware of my spiritual walk. Lazarus' influence was necessary for a season, but not indefinitely. After a period of being dependent on Lazarus, God showed me that I had to let go. And when I did, I got closer to God. Now, I work and pray unto God and no man, or as Jesus told the Pharisees, "Render unto Caesar that which is Caesars' and unto God that which is God's!"

No More Anxiety Attacks/Strategy to Win

My anxiety attacks no longer torment me. I merely "brace myself" for the impact, which is nothing like it used to be. I'm no longer afraid of Satan because I understand and believe that God is in control and His word reassures it. "If I be for you, who can be against you!" it says. I don't enjoy walking into sin but the appetite of my flesh sometimes gets the best of me.

Romans Chapter 7 encourages me that Jesus Christ is my remedy against temptation. Something someone shared with me might help you visualize how we fight in the spirit. God's word tells us that we may get angry but don't sin. So how do we overcome anger without sinning? As I said earlier, I would rather be angry than afraid, but now I understand where to direct my anger. When the spirit of anger tries to overwhelm me, the word of God is my defense. When you speak the word of God, your tongue is metaphorically a double-edged sword. In this case, speaking the word cuts the enemy and backs him off you. As you repeat the word of God, you resist the attack of the enemy and faith takes over to drive that demon back to hell.

Can you imagine the world if 90 percent of the population believed and understood the word of God? Satan knows this and that's why he likes when people feel that ignorance is bliss.

I remember my battle with fear like it was yesterday. The spirit of fear relentlessly attacked me until I spoke the word of God against it. I found the scripture that says, "I have not given you a spirit of fear, but of love, power, and a sound mind." It wasn't until I believed in the words I spoke that I experienced peace, love and a sound mind.

We must understand that our minds are battlefields for God's Holy Spirit and Satan's demons. When we allow the Holy Spirit to guide and defend us, we learn how to fight against sin, temptation, and evil.

Use your imagination to understand what I'm saying. This is a conversation between me and the spirit of doubt.

Evil spirit: "There's no use for you to feel confident in yourself."

Me: "My confidence is in the Lord."

Evil spirit: "Don't you realize that people in your neighborhood carry guns?"

Me: "God says no weapon formed against me shall prosper."

Evil spirit: "Come on, you know you're going to flip out again and go back to the hospital."

Me: "God has not given me the spirit of fear, but of love, power, and a sound mind."

Evil spirit: "You're in this battle by yourself. No one can save you."

Me: "God says He sticks closer than a brother."

Each time the evil spirit attacks with his lies and deception in the spirit world, I speak the word of God and my tongue is that double-edged sword that strikes back. That is why we should read the word of God and get more understanding of its edification and support. The evil spirit can only bring temptation, doubt, fear, insecurity, dread and poverty to discourage what God planted into our lives. But the devil is a liar! God gives us power and knowledge against the enemy through His word and from His grace, which is why we are to meditate in God's word daily. The more you know, the better equipped you'll be and the less likely the enemy's effectiveness will be on you. Remember, when the enemy speaks in your mind, you speak the word of God back to him. I pray that we will all do like the Apostle Paul and "fight the good fight."

Let me reiterate how Jesus fights our battles. The Holy Spirit is there with me in battle. I'm covered in the armor of God with a helmet of salvation. My chest is covered with the breastplate of righteousness. My loins girted with truth. My feet shod with boots prepared for the gospel of peace. I have a shield of faith to block the fiery darts of Satan. Finally, I have that ever reliable double-edged sword. Every verse, scripture, and word of God, is engraved on the sword as a reminder of how powerful this weapon is.

We must be careful though. This flesh can get us in trouble. The Lord said, *"In the flesh dwelleth no good thing."* Our flesh cannot be prayed to. We cannot call out to it in battle or believe in it. It is useless in spiritual warfare. It is the one thing that causes us to fall in battle and to be bound in spiritual chains. When this happens, we become vulnerable during the attacks of Satan's demonic forces. Thank God for the Holy Spirit that resides in us and that Jesus intervenes on our behalf.

In many cases, some results can only come through fasting and prayer. So we turn down our food for a time and read the word of God more intently while remaining in a posture of prayer. We turn off the television and internet, removing any negative influences to clear our minds. For me, the word of God strengthens me and in it reveals his power and purpose. So I cry out to the name of Jesus. Now the demonic forces behold the power of God as I glow in my full armor of God.

Demons: "Uh oh!"

Me: "HALLELUJAH!"

When we speak in other tongues, as the Spirit gives utterance, we exemplify true redemption. It is another weapon in our defense and offense on the enemy who is confused and thrashed by the angels that do battle on our behalf. The demons that sought to torment me were cast back to hell.

Finally, my mind was clear. I looked down at the chains that had fallen off and marveled. How could these small chains have kept me bound? I came to the understanding that they were flimsy and in an instant they dissolved into the calm breeze of tranquility.

Now I am able to walk a much clearer path because I understand the foolishness that the enemy attacked me with. I see and look forward to the prize of salvation, peace, love, joy, strength, and any other good thing that God has for me to be blessed and to be a blessing.

Getting Grounded

To know God better, I had to read the Bible, fast, and pray. I needed a church that preached the word of God concerning Jesus Christ. This has enlightened me for many years and I have grown to learn, understand, and love God more. Sometimes my rage against the evil of Satan forces me to boast about Jesus. His word tells us to be swift to hear, slow to speak, and slow to wrath. This verse, found in James Chapter 1, has helped me to respond to negative situations in a positive way. Learning scriptures, studying them and applying them to my life have elevated my spirit and increased my awareness of evil. It is always good to be in God's presence. Deciding to follow God makes that person great in God's eyes. "All things work together for good to those who love the Lord and are called to his purpose."

As I gain knowledge, wisdom, and understanding, I am able to visualize the words I read. God has also blessed me with the talent of drawing so as I read what may be difficult for some, I draw images that can better illuminate their meaning.

When I feel the presence of evil or come face to face with a demon, I often ignore how it looks and recognize what it says. To some, recognizing a demon's presence can be scary but to know that the love and power of the almighty God is greater than every unclean spirit causes us to swell with courage and spiritual aggression.

Naturally, we take our fighting posture against the evil and anger may accompany us, but the peace of God stays within us.

I understand more about my life, my purpose, and my calling now than ever before. In a world of madness, God called me and many others to His purpose and pleasure. The security guard job that I was terminated from meant less and less to me as time went on, even though I still remember how it made me feel.

I found that Christ gives me the ability to accomplish anything. The Bible says I can do all things through Christ who strengthens me. The demons knew Jesus and the Apostle Paul, but now they know me as well. I am informing the enemy that I stand firmly on God's side.

SURRENDERED TO GOD

I have successfully surrendered to the knowledge of God to declare the works of the Lord and allowed His power to destroy the works of the enemy. I realize that there will be future battles, but I have a greater appreciation for the scripture that says, "If God is for me, who can be against me?" After my last battle, I was a little reluctant to face more demonic pestilence and temptation, but I had an uncanny sense of courage. Storms seemed inevitable so I had to remind myself where my strength came from and I definitely knew not to bite the hand that fed me. Storms also gave me immense gratitude to God because they forced necessary changes in my character and personality. Above all, it allowed me to see God's grace and mercy on me. After storms, my only concerns were if the next one would be as intense and whether I would have the strength to overcome it. I was forced to trust in the Lord or continue having panic attacks. I learned to trust the Lord. I am convinced that if people could see their futures, they would avoid conflict or struggle but also lead eventless lives without developing their areas of weakness. They also wouldn't need the one who created them.

What would we do if we felt we had no need to acknowledge God? Throughout the ages of mankind, we see that our hearts are filled with lust and wicked desires. Through the word of God we also see the redemption of mankind with knowledge, wisdom and understanding.

It's only reasonable for man to seek out his beginning and learn what is acceptable in moral decorum. Throughout the Bible, man has evolved from pagan savagery to order and discipline by the guidance and will of God. We also know that God had to reject evil from his presence, hence the fall of Lucifer. We must also understand that the evil of this world condemned us to evil until God sent his son, Jesus Christ, to redeem us and save the very thing that initiates our very being and purpose. The only thing that prevents us from reaching our full potential is our free will. Many people choose wickedness of worldly systems rather than the things of God. Our flesh is our weakness but our spirit is our guide, as long as it is God's Holy Spirit.

Anger and Frustration/Battling Again

There are times when I am battling my flesh that I am hit with numerous thoughts and emotions. I try to ignore the very thing that makes me feel good but leads me to sin. Ultimately, it leads me to frustration and anger. Apostle Paul wrote in the book of Romans that this happens to everybody who seeks God's glory. As long as I know that God is with me, I gain strength to continue pursuing his will for my life. Satan knows that God is my protection but he continues to tempt me. The Holy Spirit helps me persevere and overcome the devils' attacks, even when it gets difficult.

When I am fighting temptation or indulgences of the flesh, I become aggressive. As a black man, I come face to face with racial issues that many black people encounter. My natural response to such issues is usually resentment, anger, or aggression towards white people. But to those who are in the spiritual fight, God says don't be a respecter of persons. Therefore, circumstances should not lead me to use evil for evil, though in worldly perspectives I might be justified. What comforts me and many others like me is that

God is in control over the situation trying our hearts and keeping us focused on him and his righteousness. Remember, however, that God's word ensures us that He does not tempt us with evil because He is not evil. Instead, our free will to *"choose ye this day which master you will serve"* is God's way of giving us the option of good or evil. If anger is the result of a racial issue, what I do with my anger is the key? I like to think before I react, but I often find myself entertaining vengeful thoughts against the person that offended me. In cases like this, these thoughts cause more damage than good. I thank God for my choice to lift weights or take a step back to think about the possibilities and consequences of my actions, which allows me to deal with my anger in a socially acceptable manner.

GIVING GOD THE GLORY

As I said before, Lazarus had a profound and lasting effect on my life and I am eternally grateful for his influence. Therefore, I thank God for him and the way he allowed God to work through him. In addition to his words of wisdom, Lazarus redirected my attention toward my dad and his unique characteristics of humility. When my parents separated, my siblings and I stayed with our mother. After their divorce, my dad had visitation rights so we mostly saw him on the weekends. Living with my mom, we gave ear to her side of their calamitous relationship which had an abstruse effect on my opinion concerning my dad's "mistreatment" of her. My mom told us bits and pieces of their relationship but it wasn't until recently that I learned my dad's perspective, although he didn't say much. What really struck me was that my dad has never sad and never expressed any negative comments about my mom. I found this to be incredibly commendable so I must acknowledge my dad's loyalty to my mom. I believe I get that trait from him and I see this loyalty in my siblings as well. My mom never gives up in a fight, whether it's physical, spiritual, or emotional. I commend her in giving that to us.

I spent most of my life trying not to be like my dad, overlooking many of his attributes, including his humility. I never realized that God smiled on humility and that my dad, despite not being perfect, had an abundance of it.

"Train up a child in the way he should go and when he is older he will not part from it." I thank my mom and dad for raising us in the church. I thank God for them both.

My dad's perspective in his relationship with my mom is brief but I understand a lot more now that I am a man. I understand why I treated women so well in my past relationships. I always gave them the attention they wanted and needed. Most of them were not wise enough to accept it because of past relationships.

My dad showed me that a man had to have integrity. I am grateful and respect him for that.

My Family

In 1968, my dad enlisted in the Navy during the Vietnam War. After completing his tour of duty, he returned to the States and married my mother. Most of us can remember the atmosphere during the 1960s and 1970s in these United States, so let me explain my dad's issues that he didn't talk about until I was in my early 20s. Though heavily burdened, my dad refused to tell me about the effects of "Agent Orange" on him and many other soldiers. Years later, he was diagnosed with paranoid schizophrenia and other chemical imbalances. During my childhood, he spent many months in the VA Hospital trying to maintain his sanity while raising a family. We lived in a predominantly white neighborhood in the 1970s called Garden City. As time went on, I saw my parent's marriage deteriorate with arguments and fights.

As a child, I never understood why a couple would fight if they loved each other so I spent most of my childhood trying to figure that out. My dad fought my mother until she left him. I was too young to understand why he acted the way he did. I was torn in my heart seeing my dad hit my mom so my love for her outweighed any reasoning my dad could remotely explain.

As I reflect on those awful days, I add the pieces of the puzzle together. My dad failed to mention the racism and bigotry on the jobs he resigned or was terminated from. He never told me about the pressure of being one of three black families on the entire block of our neighborhood and the prejudice attitudes from our white neighbors that he had to endure. He never told me how hard it was raising four children and supporting his wife while encountering horrific flashbacks and paranoid delusions. He never told me how hard it would be to hold on to your faith in God in a relentless, cold, harsh world. He didn't have to tell me any of this because my life in many ways reflected his. Enduring the stresses of life is one thing but a mental disorder doesn't simplify it in any way.

When I talked to my dad, my heart went out to him because I am him and he was me. The love I have for my mother is still strong and I can't leave out that she always told us to respect our dad even if we didn't understand him. I loved my parents equally because I understand they did the best they could while living their lives and making lives for us. They both started us in God's way and we still acknowledge God in all our ways. God directs my path and I honor my parents for this. My current lifestyle has been anything but premeditated.

I asked my wife's hand in marriage on February 23, 2014, one day after my dad passed. Her daughter, Bre'ah, and youngest son, Justice, now call me dad. My spouse and I have a radio talk show called, Serene Motivations Radio that glorifies God and applies His word to contemporary aspects of everyday life. We are also joint business owners of an illustration/transformational speaking company. I have written three books and illustrated five children's books. I am happy to say that I am a better person because of everything I've been through. I know that God is not done with me but I've come a long way. I'm looking forward to what God is going to do next.

When I was first prescribed medications I was put on high dosages of Depakote, Prozac, Haldol, Trilafon, Lithium, Clozaril, etc. Seroquel had been my final prescription at 900mg. I am currently at 100mg and one day soon will be completely independent of all meds. With my wife, who is the love of my life, my children, the talent that God gave me, and the Holy Spirit, I know that I will make it. God has proven himself in my life over and over again and continues to remain praiseworthy. I pray that every person that I encounter from this day forward will see my light shine so they may seek and glorify our Father, God in heaven.

ABOUT THE AUTHOR

Terrelle T. Lewis is an accomplished artist and writer who desires to impact the world with his gifts. Co-host of Serene Motivations Radio Show on the Survival Radio Christian Network, Terrelle shares his journey to show people that you never have to accept where you are when you dream of something better. He resides in Pittsburgh, PA, with his wife, Johnnette, and their children.

VISIT EX3 BOOKS
FOR OTHER TITLES

www.EX3ent.com

Leave your comments and reviews of Manic: Through Hell and Back at ExpectedEndEntertainment@gmail.com, EX3ent.com or on Amazon.com.